BEST

TRAIL RUNS

DENVER, BOULDER & COLORADO SPRINGS

ADAM W. CHASE | NANCY HOBBS | PETER JONES

FALCONGUIDES®

GUILFORD, CONNECTICUT

An imprint of Globe Pequot

Falcon and FalconGuides are registered trademarks and Make Adventure Your
Story is a trademark of Rowman & Littlefield.

Distributed by NATIONAL BOOK NETWORK
Copyright © 2017 Rowman & Littlefield

Maps: Melissa Baker © 2017 Rowman & Littlefield

British Library Cataloguing in Publication Information available

Library of Congress Cataloging-in-Publication Data available

ISBN 978-1-4930-2341-7 (paperback)
ISBN 978-1-4930-2342-4 (e-book)

♾™ The paper used in this publication meets the minimum requirements of
American National Standard for Information Sciences—Permanence of Paper for
Printed Library Materials, ANSI/NISO Z39.48-1992.

Printed in the United States of America

Colorado Springs Runs   **136**

INTRODUCTION

INTRODUCTION

SEVERAL WELL-WRITTEN AND THOROUGHLY RESEARCHED TRAIL RUNNING GUIDEBOOKS FEATURE COLORADO TRAILS, and there are even more hiking guides for the same territory—and really, what is the difference between the two when it comes to choosing a guide? With so many resources already available to trail runners seeking enticing trails to explore, what distinguishes this one?

We didn't undertake this project because we thought we could do a "better" job than our friends before us but, rather, because we thought we'd bring new trails to light and that our presentation of the trails we've selected would be written from a different and more current perspective. It is our aim to provide you with fresh, new trails to go with traditional, sure-bet, can't-miss runs for the Front Range between Colorado Springs and Boulder. We live here, we run here, and we love these trails and want to share them with you.

It has been our aim, either through *The Ultimate Guide to Trail Running* or our roles with the American Trail Running Association, to help hikers accelerate and become trail runners, assist road runners to convert and adapt to trails, and provide direction for current trail runners to become stronger, more agile, and efficient. While we've been able to tackle the "how" in past work, this book allows us to take on the "where."

Trail Running 101 to Postdoc

DIFFICULTY RATINGS

Being that many trail runners are also Alpine skiers who understand the meaning of easy/green, intermediate (moderate)/blue, and difficult/black for rating the difficulty of a run, we chose to go with that for the trails in this book. We acknowledge the subjective nature of this, noting that one person's hard is another's easy, but we did want to guide readers with some sense of relative ease or difficulty so that they may plan accordingly.

CELL PHONE COVERAGE

We also deemed it helpful to readers to know if a trail has cell phone coverage. This is merely for safety purposes. We urge trail runners to use proper etiquette and to refrain from using phones, except in cases of emergency or to take pictures of the beautiful scenery through which these trails run.

Getting Started

Whereas road running is a more straightforward, linear function, trail training is multidimensional, because it blends lateral motion with forward movement. To adapt your training routine to accommodate the varying terrain inherent on trails, you will need to focus on strengthening your stabilizing muscles and balance. Similarly, because you will surely encounter hills—both steep and steady climbs—as a trail runner, you should consider the benefits of including training workouts that focus on strength, such as running hill repeats of varying intervals and distance. If you want to become a faster and fitter trail runner, you should consider increasing your speed through repeats, improving your fitness by running intervals and speed drills, and, finally, you may want to hit the weight room and incorporate a stretching regime.

Trail Training

Compared with road running, trail running requires a more balanced and comprehensive approach, incorporating the whole body. Trail runners must be prepared to handle varying terrain, conditions, steep inclines and declines, and other challenges not found on the road. Fortunately, one thing trail runners don't need to train for is dealing with motorized vehicles.

Although many of the following training techniques apply to road running, it is also necessary to perform them on trails if your goal is to become a better, more accomplished trail runner. Yes, you may become a faster road runner by doing speed work on the track; but that speed does not always transfer to trails, where you will be forced to use a different stride, constantly adjust your tempo for frequent gear changes, and maintain control while altering your body position to stay upright.

Distance Training

If your goal is to run or race a certain distance, then training for that distance will be a mandatory building block in your trail training regimen. Incorporating long runs into weekly training will help your body adjust physiologically to increased impact-loading stress by generating more bone calcium deposits and building more and stronger leg muscles and connective tissue. Building weekly mileage improves your aerobic capacity to build a base upon which you can mix speed and strength training runs into your schedule.

Long training runs enable your body to cope with high mileage by breaking down fats for fuel and becoming more biomechanically efficient. Psychologically, long runs teach you to cope with and understand fatigue. During lengthy training runs, runners frequently experience what can become an emotional roller coaster. It is useful to become familiar with how you respond under such circumstances, especially if you are training for a long-distance trail race. Long runs also help build confidence as a measure of progress. And, perhaps best, these runs become adventures into unchartered territory, allowing you to explore new stretches of trails and see new sights.

Some simple advice for those converting from roads to trails—especially for those who keep a log to record time, distance, and pace—is to forget about training distance or, if you know the distance of a trail, leave your watch behind when you go for a training run. Since trail running is invariably slower than road running, you will only get frustrated if you make the common mistake of comparing your trail pace with your road or track pace.

A prime reason for running trails is to escape tedious calculations, so free yourself from distance or time constraints and just run and enjoy, particularly during your initial exposure to trail running. Tap into the wonderful feeling of breezing by brush and trees as you flow up and down hills and maneuver sharp corners with skill and agility. You can always fret about your pace as you develop your trail skills and speed.

If you base your trail running training on the premise that long runs are primarily a function of time rather than ground covered, you should keep training runs close to the amount of time you think it will take to run your target distance. For example, if you are training to complete a 5-mile trail run in the near future, you might set your training run for 45 minutes. If, however, you are training for a trail marathon or ultramarathon, you probably want to keep your distance training to somewhat less than the time it will take you to complete the race distance. To get to that point, you may want to set aside between one day every two weeks to two days a week for long runs, depending on your goal, experience, fitness background, and resistance to injury.

Trail runners usually dedicate one day of the week for a considerably longer training run, although some prefer to run two back-to-back relatively long days, especially on weekends when their schedules are more accommodating. This latter training method, known as a "brick workout," is common among ultramarathoners, who must condition their bodies to perform when tired and stressed. Newer runners should not try brick workouts until they are comfortable with trails and are confident that their bodies will be able to withstand two days of long runs without breaking down or suffering injury.

Because of the forgiving surface of trails, which may allow a person to run relatively injury-free, newer trail runners are often lulled into building up their distance base with long runs too rapidly. Whether performed on road or trail, distance running takes its toll on the body; and too quick an increase in distance often leads to injury, burnout, or leaving your body prone to illness due to a compromised immune system. Depending on age, experience with endurance athletics in general, and your running history, it is better to increase your mileage, or hours per week, by no more than 5 percent to 10 percent per week.

Even if you increase your mileage base gradually, do not forfeit quality for quantity. Many runners succumb to the unhealthy game of comparing weekly mileage with either their previous weeks or the mileage of other runners. Junk miles are just that. Depending on your objectives, it is usually better to run fewer miles with fresher legs and at a more intense pace than to slog through miles merely to rack them up in your logbook.

One way to check the quality of your miles is to wear a heart rate monitor, and couple the distance of your runs with the goal of staying within your training zone at a steady pace. If you find your heart rate consistently rising above or falling below that target rate as you tack on the miles, that is a sign you are overtraining, and it is unlikely you will derive much benefit from those miles unless you are training for ultradistance.

Speed Training

For some trail runners, just being out on the trails and communing with nature is enough. They don't care about pace. Building up your distance base should help to increase running speed, but it only helps to a certain extent. To really pick up speed and break through the barrier of your training pace, you should run fast. Running at a faster pace helps improve both cardiovascular fitness and biomechanical efficiency. This discussion, however, is aimed at those who find it more exhilarating to push their limits, who enjoy the feeling of rushing along a wooded path, and who appreciate the fitness improvements that result from challenging themselves.

Beyond velocity, speed training—whether through intervals, repeats, tempo runs, fartleks, or other means—has positive physiological effects. Pushing the pace forces muscles and energy systems to adapt to the more strenuous effort of speed training. The body does this by improving the flow of blood to muscles, increasing the number of capillaries in muscle fiber, stimulating muscles to increase their myoglobin and mitochondria content, and raising aerobic enzyme activity to allow muscles to produce more energy aerobically.

Running fast also provides a mental edge because, psychologically, if you are familiar with the stress and burning sensation known to many as "pain and suffering," which accompanies running at a faster-than-normal pace during training, you will be able to draw from that experience and dig deeper into your reserves when needed during a race. Speed training on trails also forces you to push your comfort level with respect to the risk of falling or otherwise losing control on difficult terrain. Pushing the envelope helps establish a sense of confidence that is crucial to running difficult sections, especially descents, at speed.

Breaking away from the daily training pace and pushing yourself shakes up the routine and rejuvenates the muscular, energy, and cardiovascular systems so that you may reprogram for a faster pace with more rapid leg speed and foot turnover. Running at a quicker pace helps realign running form and teaches respect for different speeds.

However, because speed training is an advanced form of training, it should not be introduced into your routine before establishing a consistent training base. Beginning trail runners should become comfortable with running on trails before they endeavor to run those trails fast. Speed training stresses the body so it may be wise to do your faster workouts on tamer trails with dependable footing, on dirt roads, or even on a track or paved road.

INTERVALS

Although interval training improves leg speed, its primary goal is cardiovascular—to optimize lactate threshold. As an anaerobic training tool, intervals are designed to increase your ability to maintain a fast pace for a longer period of time. Without an improvement in lactate threshold, a runner will be unable to run or race a substantial distance at a faster pace than the rate at which the body can comfortably use oxygen, thereby causing lactate to form in the bloodstream. Intervals help to raise the level at which the body begins the lactate production process, so that you are able to run faster and longer without feeling muscles burn or cramp. Upon developing a substantial training base of endurance, speed intervals allow acceleration of pace and an increase in overall running fitness.

Intervals are usually measured in terms of time rather than distance, especially if run on hilly or rugged trails. During the "on" or hard-effort segments of interval training, trail runners should work hard enough to go anaerobic (i.e., exceed the lactate or anaerobic threshold so that the body goes into oxygen debt). During the "off" or recovery segments, you are allowed to repay some of the oxygen debt, but not all of it. The rest period should be sufficiently short so that you are "on" again before full recovery.

An interval workout may be a series of equal on-and-off interval and recovery periods, or a mix of intervals and recoveries of different lengths. For example, a trail runner might run six intervals of four minutes each interspersed with three-minute recoveries. Alternatively, the interval session might mix it up with five-, four-, three-, two-, three-, four-, and five-minute intervals, each separated by a three-minute recovery.

Intervals may be as long as six minutes and as short as 30 seconds. Run intervals at a pace that is a bit faster than lactate threshold, which is usually equivalent to the pace run when racing a distance from 2 miles to 5 kilometers in length. The interval pace should be uncomfortable, but not excruciating; although not a sprint, you should feel you are running fast.

Run longer intervals if training for longer distances, and shorter intervals if speed is the goal. The off or recovery period between intervals is an active rest that ranges from jogging to moderate running. Recovery time should be a little shorter than the length of the interval preceding it. In addition to recoveries between the intervals, any interval workout should integrate a substantial warm-up and cooldown.

HILL REPEATS AND REPETITION WORKOUTS

"Repeats" resemble intervals, except that leg speed and strength are emphasized more than lactate threshold (although repetition workouts have some beneficial lactate threshold effects). Put another way, repeat workouts are designed for biomechanical and physiological improvement more than for cardiovascular benefits. Hill repeats are intended to hone your climbing skills, and generally make for a stronger runner by taxing the muscular system with anaerobic intervals.

Repeats are run at or faster than the lactate threshold pace, and each interval is shorter in length than a standard interval workout. Typically, repeats last two minutes or less; and because repeats are more intense than intervals, the recovery period is longer. Since the focus is muscle strength improvement rather than fitness, the active rest between repeats should be long enough to recharge and prepare for the next repeat at or above lactate threshold. In short, if you run a two-minute repeat and need three minutes to recover, take the full three minutes. You want to recover enough to make each repeat interval sufficiently intense to realize the full benefits of the exercise.

Run each interval at a pace that you can maintain through the entire repeat workout. Don't push so hard during early repeats that you are unable to finish the rest of the workout. Hill repeats provide a great strength and lactate threshold workout with minimal stress to the body, because you push hard to go anaerobic while climbing, but then rest as you slowly jog or walk to the bottom of the hill. Because of the reduced stress, you can throw hill repeats into training schedule on a weekly basis without jeopardizing the health of connective tissue.

TEMPO RUNS

Imagine a spectrum, with repeats that focus on biomechanics and muscular strength buildup at one end, then intervals that focus on a combination of lactate threshold and biomechanics in the middle, and tempo runs at the other end that emphasize lactate threshold or cardiovascular fitness.

Repeats	Intervals	Tempo Runs
Biomechanics/Strength		Cardio/Lactate Threshold

Tempo runs are sustained efforts at an even pace, usually lasting about 20 to 40 minutes, although those training for longer distances may do tempo runs that stretch to 90 minutes. The pace should be a lactate threshold pace, which is faster than the pace at which you are able to maintain a conversation, but not faster than one that forces you to exceed 90 percent of your maximum heart rate. The pace can be maintained for about an hour, if racing. Since the goal of tempo training is to maintain a steady pace with consistent leg turnover, run tempos on a trail or dirt road that is relatively flat, with good footing.

Tempo runs should include a warm-up and cooldown, both at a comfortable pace. If the tempo workout involves training partners, be careful to not turn the session into a race or time trial. To prevent that from occurring, wear a heart rate monitor and set it to sound an alarm if the heart rate rises above lactate threshold rate. Because tempo runs are physiological workouts, the goal is to run at a certain effort rather than to cover a certain distance. Depending on terrain, weather, or how rested you are the pace may vary, but the body should nevertheless be working at threshold level throughout the workout.

Because considerable concentration and focus is required to maintain a steady lactate threshold pace for 20 minutes or longer, runners frequently find themselves a bit tired, both physically and mentally, for a day or two after a tempo workout. If that is the case, take a day of active rest or work a recovery run into your schedule. It may even be advisable to take the next day off to rest up and maintain trail running vigor.

FARTLEKS

Fartlek is Swedish for "speed play." Scandinavians, known for their trail running prowess and long history in the sport, pioneered the art of running fast on trails. Fartleks are creative workouts that weave a variety of paces into the same run. Although fartleks can be performed solo, they are often run as a group in single file with the leader setting the pace—sometimes sprinting, sometimes jogging, sometimes walking, at other times simply running. Because the pace of a fartlek often varies with the terrain, these invigorating workouts are most successful if run on trails that offer a mix of short and long hills and plenty of turns and obstacles.

Fartleks offer a fun alternative to more standardized, timed speed workouts. Because they lack any regimented order, fartleks can reinject zip into a training routine that has grown boring, or introduce some excitement when running feels lethargic. The pacesetter can rotate, and faster runners may loop back to pick up stragglers to keep the fartlek group intact.

To capture some benefits of a fartlek when running alone, throw in some surges to get some speed training. Surges are short blasts of speed worked into a training run to accentuate a transition in the trail, such as near the top of a hill or when reaching the bottom of a hill and beginning a climb.

Another way to mix training with a little speed is to integrate striders or accelerations into the routine. An excellent time to insert striders or accelerations is at the end of a trail run, just before the cooldown. Striders and accelerations are usually performed on flat, soft surfaces such as grassy parks, playing fields, or dirt roads. If striders or accelerations are run on grass or sand, try removing shoes to work on the muscle tone of the lower legs and feet while feeling light and free in these speed workouts. Strider and acceleration distances should range between 50 and 100 meters, allowing for an additional 10 meters to get started and 20 to 30 meters to slow down.

A strider is usually run at a fast pace, just under or even finishing with a sprint. Place emphasis on high knee lifts and getting a full kick off each step to cover as much ground as possible without overstriding. When striding, think of sprinters warming up on a track, swinging arms and lifting knees in an accentuated manner. Accelerations resemble striders, but begin more slowly and end in a full sprint.

"OFF-TRAIL" SPEED TRAINING

Although the goal of speed training is to improve physiolog, the cardiovascular system, biomechanics, the muscular system, and mental strength, it is not necessary to do all speed training on trails. In fact, it is more effective to perform some speed training sessions on the track, dirt, or even paved roads. Depending on where you live and the types of trails to which you have access, it may be a lot easier to do speed training off the trails, reserving the trip to trails for longer runs.

Road and track are better suited for certain types of speed training. Tempo runs, where the focus is on a steady pace, and repeats, where the emphasis is on leg turnover, should be performed on flatter, more dependable surfaces. Roads or tracks are certainly easier than trails for these types of workouts, especially if trails are icy or muddy.

Track sessions tend to be highly efficient. Perhaps it is the lane lines or the bends of the turns, but something about running on a track creates a feeling of running fast. That feeling may well convert to actual speed, which means a more effective speed session. Tracks are also measured for convenient pacing. If you want to do repeats or intervals and maintain a set pace, going to the track is an efficient alternative to the trail.

In addition to selecting the appropriate speed workout and venue to perform the session, also take the weather into consideration. If it is snowy, icy, muddy, or particularly windy, it may not be possible to get a good speed workout outside. Depending on training needs and personal preferences, train inside and run a set of repeats or intervals on the treadmill, or work on leg turnover with some spinning. However, many trail runners are adamantly opposed to such mechanical alternatives and insist on running outside, regardless of the weather. That is fine and well, but they then must be willing to either forego speed training sessions when the weather is particularly nasty or attempt to do them under unfavorable conditions.

BOULDER RUNS

BOULDER RUNS

A BOLD BUT TRUE STATEMENT: "BOULDER IS THE TRAIL RUNNING CAPITAL OF THE WORLD." As such it attracts the best trail runners, and if housing were cheaper it would boast an even greater population of trail running fiends. It is also home to a large population of the world's best road runners, triathletes, climbers, cyclists, and many other athletic elites, so you never know who might run by you out on the trails. Part of the city's draw is its access to a wonderful playground, and part is its varying shades of superb weather. It is one of the sunniest places on earth and that is reflected in the demeanor of its happy residents.

Boulder's bright population sets the tone for playing host to a slew of outdoor athletic gear and apparel companies, as well as for making the city a global capital for natural foods and alternative healing. As the result of these industries being so prominent, Boulder has become an "It" city—a place to get the best gear and to enjoy healthy eating and, especially, good drinking when it comes to microbreweries.

The city boasts three strong running stores, including Fleet Feet Boulder, Flatirons Running Inc., and Boulder Running Company. And, for other outdoors needs, there is also Montbell, Neptune Mountaineering, Outdoor DIVAS, The North Face, REI, Patagonia, Title 9, Prana, lululemon, and other purveyors of adventure gear.

For food and grog, there are as many coffee shops as there are trust funders to fill their seats. For trail runner-friendly cafes, the Walnut and Southside Cafes boast hardy fare, and the list of breweries, including Mountain Sun, Southern Sun, Sanitas, Upslope, Fate, and Avery, have won as many awards as the city's trail runners have trophies on their shelves.

MOUNT SANITAS

ONE OF BOULDER'S CLASSIC TRAIL RUNS is a rather steep and, thanks to the flood of September 2013 and heavy rains in the spring of 2015, a rocky and rugged trail that ascends 1,300 feet in less than 1.5 miles. The current fastest known ascent, from the covered shelter just off Mapleton Avenue to the metal summit marker, is 14:12, set by Kilian Jornet in 2010, when he was visiting Boulder only a week after he had run the Western States 100 in California.

Just as challenging as the ascent is the perplexing decision of how to pronounce the mountain's name. There is "sahn-ee-toss," which is technically correct because the name was derived from the sanitarium housed there in the late 1800s. But that comes across as affected and overly "I'm a local and in the know." Most call it "san-EE-tis," emphasizing the "ee." Regardless, it is a jewel of a mountain, made all the more precious by the addition of a new trail on its west flank.

Boulder celebrates Mount Sanitas, which is centrally located and very easy to access, by using its trails on a frequent basis. On weekdays it is a regular dog walking and running destination, with many using the trails from the surrounding neighborhoods or from downtown. On weekends the parking lots are full, and hikers and climbers add to the mix.

MOUNT SANITAS SUMMIT

THE RUN DOWN

START: Mount Sanitas Trailhead

OVERALL DISTANCE: 3.5 miles

APPROXIMATE RUNNING TIME: 45 minutes

DIFFICULTY: Blue

ELEVATION GAIN: 1,200 feet

BEST SEASON TO RUN: Spring, summer, and fall

DOG FRIENDLY: Dogs must be on leash at trailheads; under voice and sight command along the trail

PARKING: Free

OTHER USERS: Hikers

CELL PHONE COVERAGE: Yes

MORE INFORMATION: https://bouldercolorado.gov/osmp/mount-sanitas-trailhead

FINDING THE TRAILHEAD

The trailhead is at the mouth of Sunshine Canyon, just west of Mapleton Avenue and 4th Street, where the road feeds into the canyon that leads to Gold Hill. Centennial Trailhead, which is to the west of the Sanitas Trailhead, offers additional parking and a public restroom.

RUN DESCRIPTION

From the Mount Sanitas Trailhead, where there is a covered shelter, head north and bear to the left as you begin a 1.4-mile steep climb up rocky, rough stair steps. You will cross a concrete bridge immediately beyond the shelter and then, in another 50 meters, you'll cross a wooden bridge. You may also see and smell bags of dog poop that Boulder's quasi-PC "guardians," or dog owners, so generously leave on the side of the trail, having delusionally promised themselves they'll fetch the putrid containers on the return trip. Dogs are allowed on this trail but may only be off-leash if they have a special city-issued tag, and are in voice and sight command.

The climb is steady and the footing is more challenging because of the erosion of soil or dirt that once filled in some of the spaces between the rocks, creating a spinelike stairway leading to the summit, where runners enjoy a fantastic view of Boulder and the surrounding foothills. Fortunately,

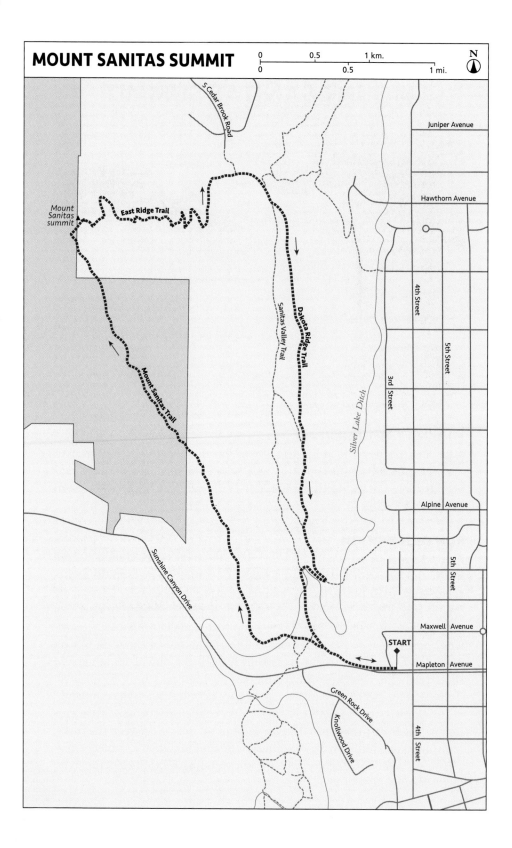

The trails on Mount Sanitas get quickly packed down in the winter. PHOTO BY TODD STRAKA

beginning in the summer of 2017, Boulder Open Space and Mountain Parks is improving the Sanitas trail, a project that may take longer than a year to complete.

To return, you may either retrace your steps or make a loop by heading down the east-facing trail, which is rather technical at the top, especially when icy or wet. But, after the first kilometer, this segues into the Sanitas Valley Trail, which was rebuilt in the summer of 2015 and now resembles a well-maintained dirt road. If you'd like to stay on singletrack, you may opt for the trail that is just east of the valley trail, called Dakota Ridge, which adds another quarter-mile to the loop.

HILLS

"FLAT TRAIL" IN THE FRONT RANGE is typically an oxymoron. True, the flat trail does exist, but given its relative rarity unless you head east of the foothills, Colorado trail runners become quickly and painfully aware of the importance and benefits of hill training.

Pacing, or economy of effort, are probably the most important aspects of effective hill running. Much to their regret, novice trail runners are frequently less inclined (no pun intended) to use appropriate pacing on hills. As a result, they face the consequences of sputtering out with burning calves, huffing lungs, and possibly even nausea long before reaching the summit. Those new to hilly trails also tend to use improper form when descending and, accordingly, suffer from aching quadriceps and knee joints.

Running hills efficiently is a skill acquired through a process of fine tuning and lots of practice, accounting for differences in body types, strengths, weaknesses, agility, fitness, and aversion to risk. Armed with proper technique, a trail runner is prepared to take on hills—or mountains, for that matter—with alacrity instead of dread.

Whether you should attack with speed or power hike a hill or steep ascent is a complex decision that depends on the length of the climb, the trail surface, your level of fatigue, the altitude, the distance of the run, at what point in the run you encounter the hill, and whether you are training or racing. Efficient power hiking is often faster than running, especially in longer runs, when the footing is difficult, or at high altitude. It can be very rewarding to hike past someone who is trying to run up a hill, and know that you are expending far less effort while you move at a faster pace. Conversely, it is quite demoralizing to be passed by a hiker while you struggle to run up a steep incline.

Two crucial elements of being a strong hill runner are tempo and confidence. A runner who is able to maintain tempo, cadence, or rhythm ascending and descending a hill is more efficient and generally faster on hills than a runner who tries to muscle up and down the same slope in fits and starts. Two secrets to maintaining your tempo on a hill is the discipline and ability to adjust stride length.

Observing the fastest and most efficient climbers, both human and animal, it is easy to note their sustained turn-over with a shortened stride on the climb. Even speedy mountain types go slower uphill and faster downhill, but the cadence of their legs hardly changes, regardless of the grade, the only difference being stride length. Just as you shift into lower gear when you bicycle up a hill, you need to shift gears as a runner by shortening your stride length.

A short stride on both the ascent and descent works very well on trails that are particularly rugged with difficult footing. By using many little steps, you will be able to make quick adjustments to correct your footing on the fly. That allows you the most sure-footed landing for better traction and control. The ability to alter your path increases both your real and perceived control, which leads to greater confidence, especially on descents. A heightened level of confidence on hills leads to a "heads-up" running style.

Proper form and confidence on hills will increase your enjoyment of inclines and declines and, at the same time, decrease the chance of injury. With more confidence, you will be able to relax and run with a lighter, more flow-ing form that is more efficient and less painful. Knowing how to confront hills will keep you coming back for more, and because training on hills, whether on long, sustained ascents or shorter hill repeats, presents a superb oppor-tunity for running-specific strength training, you will become a stronger and more confident runner overall.

MOUNT SANITAS TO LION'S LAIR

THE RUN DOWN

START: Mount Sanitas Trailhead

OVERALL DISTANCE: 5.9 miles

APPROXIMATE RUNNING TIME: 1.5 hours

DIFFICULTY: Blue

ELEVATION GAIN: 1,343 feet

BEST SEASON TO RUN: All but winter

DOG FRIENDLY: Dogs are not permitted

PARKING: Free

OTHER USERS: Hikers

CELL PHONE COVERAGE: Yes

MORE INFORMATION: https://bouldercolorado.gov/osmp/mount-sanitas-trailhead

FINDING THE TRAILHEAD

The trailhead is at the mouth of Sunshine Canyon, just west of Mapleton Avenue and 4th Street, where the road feeds into the canyon that leads to Gold Hill. Centennial Trailhead, which is to the west of the Sanitas Trailhead, offers additional parking and a public restroom.

RUN DESCRIPTION

Mount Sanitas is known to have the occasional mountain lion visit, along with coyotes, foxes, and plenty of mule deer (aka lion food). That is probably the reason why Boulder's newest—and arguably most awesome—trail is named "Lion's Lair."

Completed in the spring of 2015, the route to Lion's Lair starts to the southwest of the Centennial Trailhead on a trail that parallels Sunshine Canyon Road, heading up the canyon. Dogs are not permitted on Lion's Lair. After a mile of gradual climbing, the trail comes to a seeming end, dropping you onto a driveway that joins Sunshine Canyon. Cross the road to another driveway to the east of the road, and head up a steep embankment to the north, where the trail becomes more pronounced.

The next mile-and-a-half climbs steadily on a well-constructed trail with multiple switchbacks. You'll see two offshoot trails to the left, one a

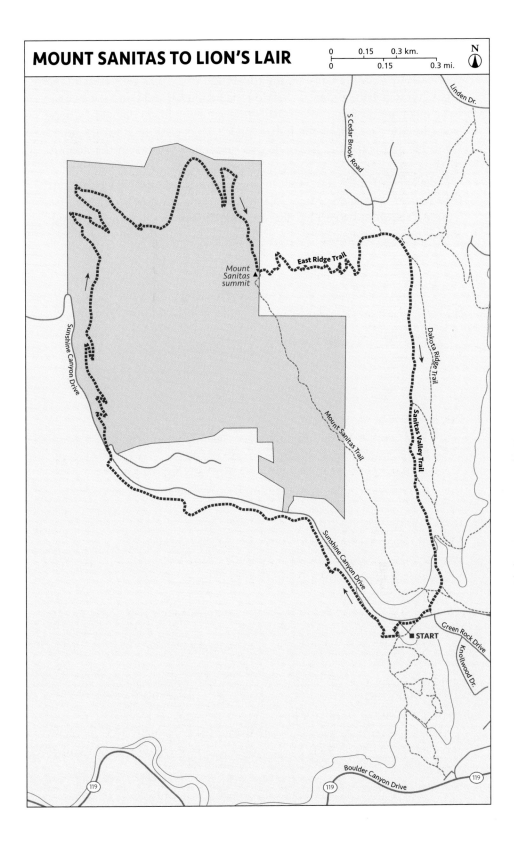

MOUNT SANITAS TO LION'S LAIR

0   0.15   0.3 km.

0   0.15   0.3 mi.

N

Linden Dr.

S Cedar Brook Road

East Ridge Trail

Mount Sanitas summit

Dakota Ridge Trail

Sunshine Canyon Drive

Mount Sanitas Trail

Sanitas Valley Trail

Sunshine Canyon Drive

Green Rock Drive

START

Knollwood Dr.

Boulder Canyon Drive

119

119

119

spur back to Sunshine Canyon, and the second at the final switchback that takes you to private property. Stay on the main trail and you'll soon come to an open meadow and, after a half-mile, a viewpoint to the west, where you can enjoy a vista of the Indian Peaks Wilderness in all of its glory. Continue on for another half-mile, and you'll find yourself at the summit of Mount Sanitas.

From the top of Sanitas, you can drop down the rocky west ridge trail for a shorter, steeper descent, or follow the eastern face down to the Sanitas Valley Trail for a longer, but more runnable way to the trailhead at the foot of the mountain.

CHAUTAUQUA PARK

CHAUTAUQUA PARK, PERCHED AS THE FOREGROUND to Boulder's iconic Flatirons, is at the top of Baseline Road, at the base of Flagstaff Mountain, the municipality's western perimeter. The parking area features a Ranger Cottage with a restroom and water fountain, and it is next to the historic Chautauqua Auditorium and a grassy meadow that is ideal for stretching and picnics. The trail network is maintained by Boulder Mountain Parks.

MESA TRAIL TO ELDORADO SPRINGS

THE RUN DOWN

START: Chautauqua Park Trailhead

OVERALL DISTANCE: 6.8 miles one way

APPROXIMATE RUNNING TIME: 1.5 hours

DIFFICULTY: Blue

ELEVATION GAIN: 1,050 feet

BEST SEASON TO RUN: Year-round, but be ready for mud in the spring, ice in the winter, and heat in the summer

DOG FRIENDLY: Dogs must be on leash at trailheads; under voice and sight command along the trail

PARKING: Free on weekdays. As of June 2017, Boulder is experimenting with providing free shuttles to Chautauqua Park on weekends, where the city will be charging for parking.

OTHER USERS: Hikers

CELL PHONE COVERAGE: Yes

MORE INFORMATION: https://bouldercolorado.gov/osmp/chautauqua-trailhead

FINDING THE TRAILHEAD

 Chautauqua Park is located at the base of the Flatirons directly off Baseline Road. Drive up Baseline Road from Broadway, Boulder's

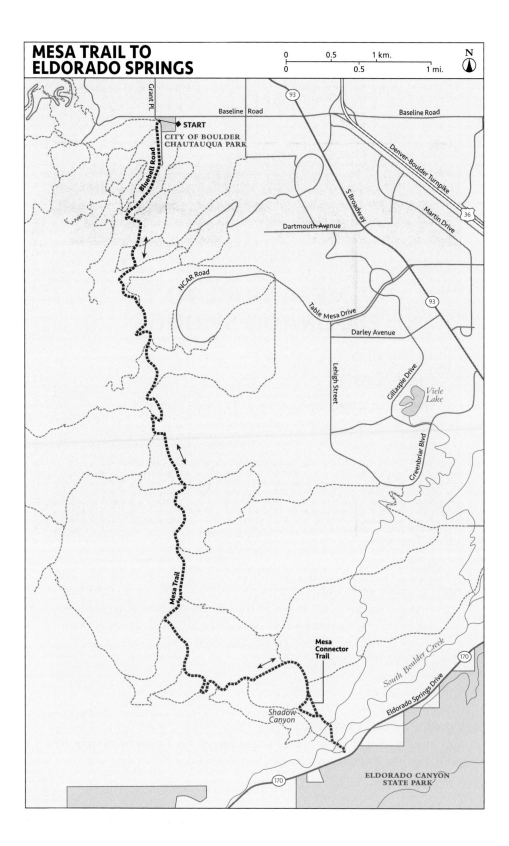

MESA TRAIL TO ELDORADO SPRINGS

0   0.5   1 km.

0   0.5   1 mi.

N

Grant Pl.

Baseline Road

Baseline Road

93

♦ START

CITY OF BOULDER
CHAUTAUQUA PARK

Bluebell Road

Denver-Boulder Turnpike

Martin Drive

36

Dartmouth Avenue

S Broadway

NCAR Road

Table Mesa Drive

93

Darley Avenue

Lehigh Street

Gillaspie Drive

Viele
Lake

Greenbriar Blvd

Mesa Trail

Mesa
Connector
Trail

South Boulder Creek

170

Shadow
Canyon

Eldorado Springs Drive

170

ELDORADO CANYON
STATE PARK

WATER CROSSINGS

Do you recall running through large puddles—or even small ponds—as a child? If so, then perhaps you mastered the technique of taking exaggerated steps with cartoonlike form, which kept you relatively dry while making everyone near you wet. That skill is invaluable for water crossings while running, and if you don't have it down take advantage of the dampness and warmth of spring to hone it. Go to a shallow stream, puddle, or other body of water that is not more than six inches deep. Think of lizards that nature programs show running in slow motion across water. Try to duplicate that high-stepping form, and throw a little lateral kick at the end of each stride to push the water away.

For deeper water crossings, decide whether it is worth trying to stay dry. The water and air temperature, the width of the body of water, the rate of any current flow, the availability of an alternative, and the amount of time you can afford should factor into your decision about where to cross. Also, remember that going around water crossings, puddles, or wet areas causes erosion.

If you don't want to take the time to keep your feet dry or to change socks, consider the "easy in/easy out" alternative. Wearing highly breathable shoes with mesh uppers allows water to penetrate when confronting water crossings; but they also allow water to exit quickly. Water will be effectively squeegeed out of the shoe by running on dry terrain, and after a mile or two a recent drenching will be only a faint memory. Wearing wool socks, especially ones made with merino wool that does not itch, will maintain a moderate temperature for your feet regardless of whether they are wet or dry. They also help prevent blisters because of their temperature-regulating attributes.

central north-south thruway, and after passing 9th Street on the right, turn left into the park entrance just across from Grant Place. There is parking in several locations around the park. As of June 2017, there will be a parking fee and limits on weekends, but parking will remain free on weekdays. All trails begin at the Ranger Cottage, located near the bottom of the large meadow at the park entrance.

RUN DESCRIPTION

THE MESA TRAIL IS BOULDER'S MOST CLASSIC RUN. There are many reasons, ranging from history, proximity, seasonal accessibility, variety, and the views it affords, but it tends to be the trail that stands out as quintessential Boulder.

MUD, SNOW, and ICE

THE BEST WAY TO DEAL WITH MUD ON THE TRAIL is to enjoy it, and to get as dirty as possible early in the run so you won't worry about it thereafter. Soft mud enables a lower impact run, especially on the descents, where mud provides a great surface for slowing the pace without stressing joints.

To avoid slipping, it may help to shorten the stride, run more upright than normal, and keep elbows more angled for lateral balance. If you begin to slip, try to relax and control the recovery so as not to overreact and fall in the opposite direction.

If water is running down the trail, your best bet is to run where water is moving most rapidly because that part of the trail will probably be the most firm. A faster current tends to remove most of the sticky sediment, leaving behind gravel and rock. Although you will get wet, the likelihood of getting bogged down on the muddier trail borders is markedly decreased. This technique is also friendlier to the trail because of the lower environmental impact.

From an environmental standpoint, resist the temptation to run alongside the trail in an effort to avoid getting muddy. Submitting to the temptation leads to wider trails, and if everyone did it, pathways would soon be major throughways instead of singletracks. A typical spring in the Front Range, with its melting snow and rain cycles, forms muddy trails and, depending on the sensitivity of the specific trail system, it may be advisable to avoid certain trails until they have a chance to dry out.

Colorado is known for its snow and, thanks to abundant sunshine and the likelihood of freezing temperatures at night, the trails of the Front Range realize a lot of ice. Running with confidence is more important on snow and ice than on any other surface. Although most runners are hesitant on snow and ice, the trick is to try to tuck away that insecurity, take a deep breath, relax, and run with a sense of command. Admittedly, snow and ice—being inanimate elements—cannot read minds, but they manage to wreak havoc on runners who fear them. Fearful runners run with tense form, lean back, and often resort to jerky, sudden movements as they attempt to adapt to the slick surface. That is just the opposite of what works best when running on slick snow or ice.

The best form for snow and ice is running with a slight forward lean that distributes the body's weight evenly across the foot as it hits the slippery surface. Fluid, steady movement is less likely to cause a loss of traction. In the event of a slip on snow or ice, the best response is to relax and to try to let your body flow with a calculated response. Do not try to stop or brake, as that will just cause you to slide out and fall. Resist the impulse to tense up or make a sudden movement to counter the slipping, which all too often leads to slipping even more. Instead, relax and breathe steadily. Even if slipping on snow and ice does lead to a fall, being relaxed will reduce the likelihood of injury. Besides, one of the best benefits of snow is that it cushions the impact.

Snowshoe and crampon or ice spike running are alternatives that make trails accessible no matter how much it snows or how much ice accumulates. The snow's forgiving compressibility and the impact absorption from snowshoes' increased surface area make it feel as though you are running on wood-chip-lined trails.

Boulder runners enjoy a tempo run on a cool winter morning.
PHOTO BY TODD STRAKA

To access the Mesa Trail, which basically runs north-to-south at the base of the Flatirons, begin at the Ranger Cottage. The parking lot fills quickly, especially on weekends. Head south from the cottage, up toward the tremendous flagstone slabs that are the five Flatirons, on a short emergency access road that leads to Bluebell Shelter, the true trailhead. From the shelter, progress past the Enchanted Mesa and Kohler Mesa trails, where you hit switchbacks to reach the NCAR (National Center for Atmospheric Research) trail junction.

Much of the Mesa Trail's undulating middle section is forested, offering plenty of shade. The trail provides access, from north to south, to Royal Arch, Bear Peak, South Boulder Peak, Fern Canyon, and Shadow Canyon. There are also options to branch off to either North or South Shanahan, as well as to the Towhee, Big Bluestem, South Boulder Creek, and Homestead Trails, before the Mesa Trail bends down to an access road and reaches its southern terminus at the South Mesa trailhead. Restrooms are located at the southern end of the trail, in the Eldorado Springs parking area.

All dogs must be leashed in the parking lot and trailhead areas. Beyond the trailhead, dogs must be on a held leash unless they meet voice and sight control standards and display a City of Boulder voice and sight tag.

GREEN MOUNTAIN

THE RUN DOWN

START: Chautauqua Park Trailhead

OVERALL DISTANCE: 6.5 miles out and back

APPROXIMATE RUNNING TIME: 2 hours

DIFFICULTY: Black

ELEVATION GAIN: 2,300 feet

BEST SEASON TO RUN: Year-round, but winter can be icy

DOG FRIENDLY: Dogs must be on leash at trailheads; under voice and sight command along the trail

PARKING: Free on weekdays, charges apply on weekends

OTHER USERS: Hikers

CELL PHONE COVERAGE: Yes

MORE INFORMATION: https://bouldercolorado.gov/osmp/chautauqua-trailhead

FINDING THE TRAILHEAD

Chautauqua Park is located at the base of the Flatirons, directly off Baseline Road. Drive up Baseline Road from Broadway, Boulder's central north-south thruway, and after passing 9th Street on the right, turn left into the park entrance just across from Grant Place. There is parking in several locations around the park. All trails begin at the Ranger Cottage, located near the bottom of the large meadow at the park entrance.

RUN DESCRIPTION

USED HISTORICALLY AS A FITNESS TEST FOR UNIVERSITY OF COLORADO NORDIC AND ALPINE SKIERS, THE RUN UP AND DOWN GREEN MOUNTAIN IS ONE OF THE MOST DIRECT ROUTES TO ONE OF THE HIGHEST POINTS ABOVE BOULDER. It is a rather intense ascent, climbing just shy of 2,300 feet in about 3 miles, and often feels like going up an odd assortment of stairs. Yet, there is something alluring about the pure effort it requires. Green's rather relentless grade lulls the brain, and attracts top athletes from a number of disciplines who make it part of their regular training regimens.

Access is via the Chautauqua trailhead. Go west on the trail that parallels Baseline Road, which is also the fortieth latitude, for a half-mile to

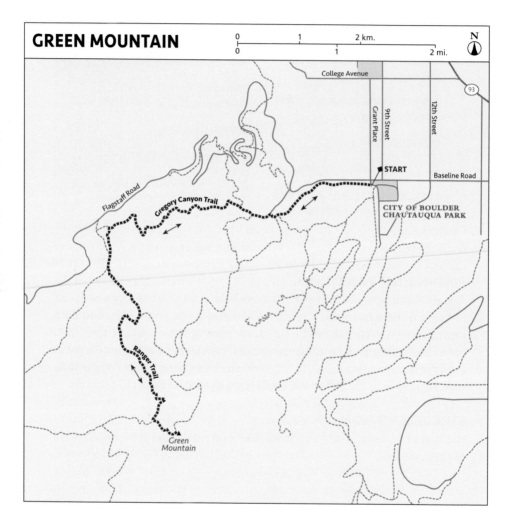

Looking up toward a cloud- and snow-covered Green Mountain from Chautauqua. PHOTO BY TODD STRAKA

Gregory Canyon. From there, continue west, through the parking area, to the Gregory Canyon Trail, where the ascent begins. In the spring, be careful to watch for poison ivy, which thrives at the canyon base. Run past the turnoff for Saddle Rock and go steadily up, to where the trail joins the Ranger Trail at about halfway up. You'll see the Green Mountain Lodge as the trail returns to the forest. Pass the E. M. Greenman Trail and bear right to stay on the Ranger Trail, which takes you through the final mile of switchbacks that drop you out on the west ridge of Bear Mountain. Take a left for the final short push to the summit, where you'll be treated to outstanding views of the Front Range, below, and Indian Peaks to the west.

From there, either backtrack for an out-and-back run, or follow the E. M. Greenman Trail to the Saddle Rock Trail to the Amphitheater Trail to the base of Gregory Canyon. This latter route is steeper but cuts off a bit of the distance.

BEAR PEAK

FINDING THE TRAILHEAD

Chautauqua Park is located at the base of the Flatirons, directly off Baseline Road. Drive up Baseline Road from Broadway, Boulder's central north-south thruway, and after passing 9th Street on the right, turn left into the park entrance just across from Grant Place. There is parking in several locations around the park. All trails begin at the Ranger Cottage, located near the bottom of the large meadow at the park entrance.

RUN DESCRIPTION

Bear Peak, Green Mountain's slightly bigger (300 feet) brother to the south, stands out as more of a true peak and, as such, is a bit of a lightning rod for athletes who live in South Boulder. One of those, our good friend Dave Mackey, had some terrible luck at the summit, and suffered an unfortunate accident when one of the huge boulders that define the very top of Bear, loosened heavy spring rains, toppled over on his leg, crushing most of it below the knee. Now the peak is a bit of an homage to Dave, and his many friends and fans cuss out the rock that did the damage. That said, Bear Peak remains a favored destination because, like Green, gaining a tremendous

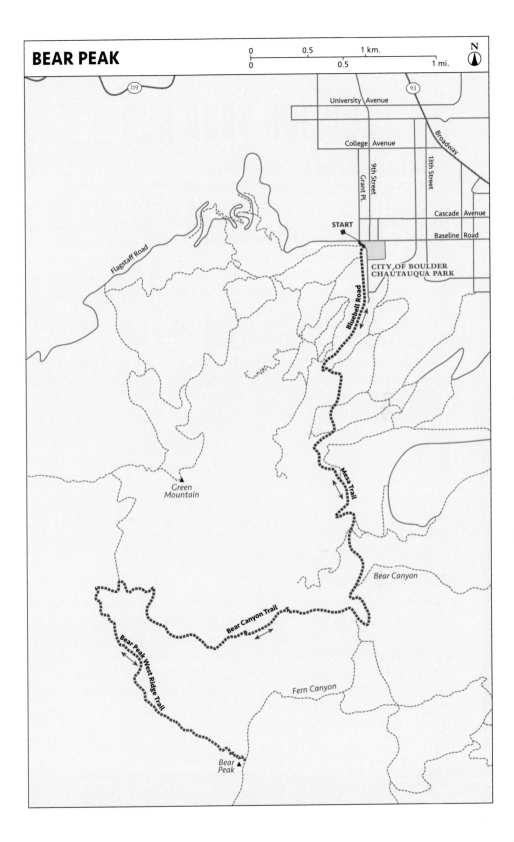

BEAR PEAK

0 0.5 1 km.
0 0.5 1 mi.

N

119

93

University Avenue

College Avenue

Broadway

9th Street

Grant Pl.

13th Street

Cascade Avenue

START

Baseline Road

Flagstaff Road

Bluebell Road

CITY OF BOULDER
CHAUTAUQUA PARK

Mesa Trail

Green
Mountain

Bear Canyon

Bear Canyon Trail

Bear Peak West Ridge Trail

Fern Canyon

Bear
Peak

FUELING YOUR RUN

WHAT TO EAT BEFORE A RUN

A PREWORKOUT MEAL SHOULD CONSIST OF MOSTLY CARBOHYDRATE-RICH foods and beverages, with a moderate amount of protein (less than 10 grams) and a small amount of fat (less than 5 grams). Eat your last meal at least two to four hours prior to a run so the body has enough time to digest and prepare itself to use stored fuel from muscle, the liver, and fat throughout the run. If you have eaten a meal and are running in less than two hours, use the principles above and just keep the meal to about 200-300 calories.

Prerun and prerace meals vary for every athlete. Some athletes are too nervous to eat solid food, so that's where endurance-type drinks and energy bars can be helpful. The key is not to eat anything different from what you normally eat during training. Race day is not the time to experiment with food.

If you run first thing in the morning, be sure to hydrate with water or a low-sugar sports drink that will settle in your stomach, and carry additional food and water as determined by the length of the run. Even a small amount of mostly carbohydrate food (100-200 calories) can improve energy levels after a full night of fasting.

Since fats and oils leave the stomach slowly, they are not suggested as a base for a preworkout diet. In fact, fat loading before exercise is unnecessary, because even thin runners have sufficient fat stored as body fat for use during exercise.

WHAT TO EAT DURING A RUN

For training or racing that lasts more than sixty minutes, it's essential to keep fueling your muscles with carbohydrates. Endurance running depletes your body's stores of carbohydrates, which must be replaced to prevent "bonking." Try to eat at regular intervals from the start of your run or competition, and don't wait until you feel tired. The duration and intensity of a trail run, along with the temperature and environmental conditions that may be encountered during the activity, are all factors in determining your nutritional and hydration needs.

Carbohydrate, not fat, is the body's most limited fuel, and is the pre-ferred fuel for the brain and nervous system. Even very lean runners have ample fat stores. However, carbohydrate is also an efficient fuel for muscles, especially at a more intense pace; the faster you go, the more you burn. In addition, the body cannot effectively burn fat for fuel unless sufficient carbohydrate exists to be broken down and drive the body's energy systems. Consuming enough carbohydrate also means the body won't have to resort to using its protein stores (the muscles) as fuel.

In general, runners who perform best are those who eat and drink con-sistently, on a plan, and maintain an even and adequate caloric intake. Liquid carbohydrate is easy to digest and enters the blood stream quick-est, but solid food can also provide a huge mental boost and stave off hun-ger pains while on the trail. In training, experiment with different types of drinks and foods so your selection is more varied, and be aware that when the intensity of running increases, your body may only tolerate liquid calories. It doesn't work to run for three or four hours and then try to back-load the calories—you'll never be able to eat enough or keep it down.

As time spent on the trail increases, include other well-tolerated solid foods, such as energy bars, cookies, watermelon, bananas, oranges, peanut butter sandwiches, turkey, and cooked potatoes, as well as liquid carbohy-drate beverages. The longer the run, the more chance the body has to break down more complex foods like these, which contain varying amounts of carbohydrate, protein, and fat, and use the energy they provide.

Bonking is an indication that the athlete is running on mere fumes. The brain is shutting the body down so no further damage occurs. In this case, quick-acting carbohydrate-rich foods, like fruit juice, soda, or sugary candy, are the only options to stabilize the body's blood sugar level. Once an athlete has bonked, special attention must be paid to fuel needs during the rest of the run or race. Carbohydrate-rich items such as sports drinks and gels, fruit and diluted fruit juice, soda, and candy (gumdrops, jelly beans, etc.) are easily absorbed and readily available for use as fuel during exercise. The best energy bars and gels are the ones that work well for, and taste good to, the individual. Find the best bar and gel through experimentation during training, and stick with it for racing. During longer runs, it's wise to have a couple of flavors to switch between, to avoid "flavor fatigue."

amount of vertical in a relatively short distance allows for sensational views over Boulder, and a real feeling of accomplishment that doesn't require a full day's effort.

From the Chautauqua Park trailhead, follow the Mesa Trail south from the Ranger Cottage (see the Mesa Trail to Eldorado Springs run description). About a half-mile after you pass to the west of the National Center for Atmospheric Research (NCAR), there is a large water tank on your left. There the trail splits; continue on the Mesa Trail, which, at this point, is a dirt road, until after a climb and a switchback, where you will see the Bear Canyon Trail branch off to the right. Follow the Bear Canyon Trail west (up) along a small stream until you reach another split, one that would take you to Green Mountain if you went to the right. Take the left, and climb up the west ridge of Bear Peak, ascending approximately 1,400 feet in approximately 2 miles. When you join the Bear Peak West Ridge Trail take a left for the final third of a mile to the rocky, exposed summit, one that really gives you the feeling like you are standing on top of a mountain—because you are, indeed, standing on top of a mountain.

From the top of Bear Peak, either turn around and run back the way you came, or head down Fern Canyon, to the east, which beelines it to the Mesa Trail, or make a longer loop by heading south toward South Boulder Peak and, at the saddle, dropping down Shadow Canyon to the south end of the Mesa Trail. If you'd prefer a shorter version of Bear Peak, you can park at NCAR: The out-and-back run is just shy of 11 miles.

FLAGSTAFF MOUNTAIN

THE RUN DOWN

START: Chautauqua Park Trailhead

OVERALL DISTANCE: 3.8 miles out and back

APPROXIMATE RUNNING TIME: 1 hour

DIFFICULTY: \Blue-Black

ELEVATION GAIN: 1,120 feet

BEST SEASON TO RUN: Year-round, but winter can be icy

DOG FRIENDLY: Dogs must be on leash at trailheads; under voice and sight command along the trail

PARKING: As of June 2017, there is an experimental weekend parking charge, but on weekdays parking is free

OTHER USERS: Hikers

CELL PHONE COVERAGE: Yes

MORE INFORMATION: https://bouldercolorado.gov/osmp/chautauqua-trailhead

FINDING THE TRAILHEAD

Chautauqua Park is located at the base of the Flatirons directly off Baseline Road. Drive up Baseline Road from Broadway, Boulder's central north-south thruway, and after passing 9th Street on the right, turn left into the park entrance just across from Grant Place. There is parking in several locations around the park. All trails begin at the Ranger Cottage, located near the bottom of the large meadow at the park entrance.

RUN DESCRIPTION

Flagstaff Mountain has a different feel from Green Mountain and Bear Peak, partly because it is smaller in stature, partly because a road goes to the top, and partly because—given the other two factors—it is more heavily traveled. It is a better-known destination for road cyclists, and the trail to the top crosses the road in five different places, each way, so runners can race bikers.

As the name implies, Flagstaff Mountain has a flagstaff at its peak, and because it looks out right over the center of Boulder and has so many access points, it has achieved deserved notoriety as being Boulder's centerpiece.

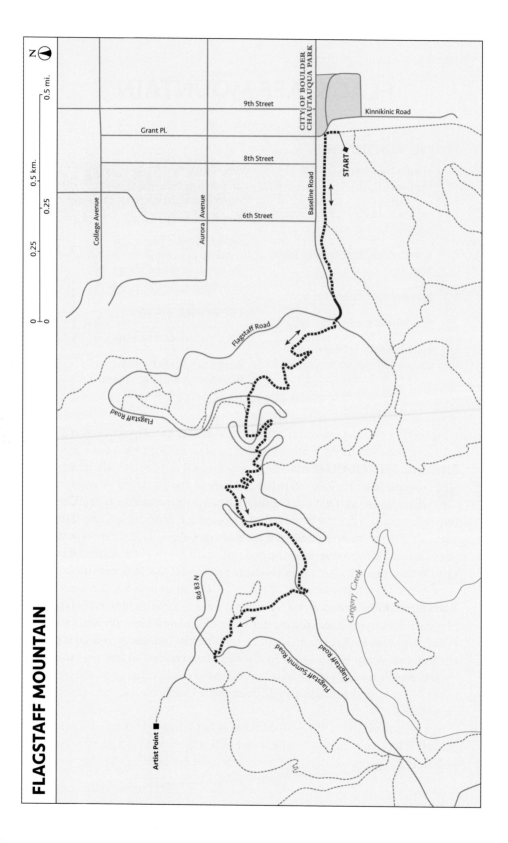

FLAGSTAFF MOUNTAIN

A runner blasts down Flagstaff Mountain toward Chautauqua Meadow. PHOTO BY TODD STRAKA

It also serves as a part of longer runs that tag a number of peaks, runs that might include Mount Sanitas, Green Mountain, and Bear and South Boulder Peaks. As such, Flagstaff is part of the Skyline Traverse, which includes all five summits.

From the Chautauqua Park trailhead, head west toward Gregory Canyon, where you'll see the Flagstaff Mountain Trail just to the right of the Gregory Canyon parking area entry. Follow the Flagstaff trail up a couple of switchbacks to the first road crossing. Continue heading up and west, and you'll soon come to two more road crossings as the trail and the road engage in rather dramatic switchbacks that serpentine across one another. You then parallel the road, before a final crossing leads to Flagstaff's false summit, where you'll see parking and a ranger station. The summit is just west of the ranger station, where there is a little berm that is the highest point in the relatively flat area. From there, you simply retrace your way back down the mountain.

BOULDER VALLEY RANCH

ONE OF THE BIGGEST ASSETS OF FRONT RANGE RUNNING is the versatility of types of running. Most of the Boulder runs in this guide are hilly, if not mountainous. Boulder Valley Ranch, however, is about as flat as it gets in Boulder and, as such, attracts quite a number of casual walkers and those seeking recovery runs. The rolling trail takes you back in time and the ranch is a working one, with cows and horses grazing in the abutting fields. Remnants of a smelter are off on the south side of the road that takes you to the trailhead.

Being a foothills city, Boulder doesn't have a reputation as being on the planes, but Boulder Valley Ranch and its groomed, dirt-road-esque trails give that impression, thanks to the prairie terrain that includes a small reservoir and views of Haystack Mountain, off to the north of the looping route. Those seeking ground for speed training or other effort runs should consider Boulder Valley Ranch, given the trail's smooth surface and lack of elevation change.

BOULDER VALLEY RANCH

THE RUN DOWN

START: Boulder Valley Ranch Trailhead

OVERALL DISTANCE: 5.4-mile loop

APPROXIMATE RUNNING TIME: 1 to 1.5 hours

DIFFICULTY: Green

ELEVATION GAIN: 750 feet

BEST SEASON TO RUN: Year-round, but mud can bog you down in winter and spring

DOG FRIENDLY: Dogs must be on leash at trailheads; under voice and sight command along the trail

PARKING: Free

OTHER USERS: Hikers, mountain bikers, equestrians

CELL PHONE COVERAGE: Yes

MORE INFORMATION: https:// bouldercolorado.gov/osmp/ boulder-valley-ranch-trailhead

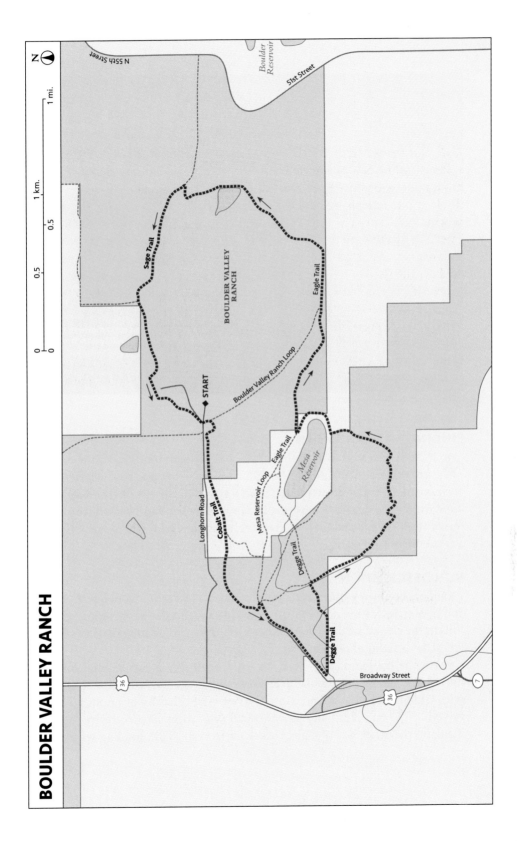

BOULDER VALLEY RANCH

N 55th Street

Boulder
Reservoir

51st Street

BOULDER VALLEY
RANCH

Sage Trail

Eagle Trail

Boulder Valley Ranch Loop

START

Longhorn Road

Cobalt Trail

Mesa Reservoir Loop

Eagle Trail

Mesa
Reservoir

Degge Trail

Degge Trail

Broadway Street

36

7

36

N

1 mi.

1 km.

0.5

0.5

0.5

0

Runners out for an early morning shakeout at Boulder Valley Ranch.
PHOTO BY TODD STRAKA

FINDING THE TRAILHEAD

The trailhead is easy to find. Take US 36 north 1 mile from the city limits, and turn right on Longhorn Road. This dirt road is often a washboard, so make sure you don't have anything that is likely to rattle loose from the vibrations it normally causes. The trailhead is at the terminus of the dirt road and there is free parking to the right, where you'll find a restroom but no water.

RUN DESCRIPTION

As a loop, Boulder Valley Ranch can be run in either direction, but if you go counterclockwise you end up coasting down what seem like bigger hills in the clockwise direction. Either way, the small climbs are relatively gradual, with one exception.

From the trailhead, head west on the Cobalt Trail, paralleling Longhorn Road, traversing grasslands as you climb gently past the intersection with Old Mill Trail a half-mile into the run. After just shy of a mile, you'll top out on Cobalt Trail and pass through two cattle gates to reach Eagle Trail, on the other side of a dirt road. Run to your right, heading west on a singletrack that parallels a dirt road on your right, until you reach the Degge Trail at the westernmost point, where there is a parking area and trailhead.

From this point, head to the east on a singletrack trail that is often muddy in the spring. Stay on that as it dips and then climbs. At 1.7 miles, after a short descent, you reach Hidden Valley Trail, where you take a right to run south. Don't be alarmed if you hear gunshots, as there is a shooting range to the south, but you may want to pick it up, as some runners have had some zingers fly past them.

Follow the singletrack as it bends to the north and passes another gate before you reach the Mesa Reservoir Trail at mile 2.7. Follow Mesa Reservoir Trail around the eastern end of the reservoir, and then take a right at Eagle Trail, passing through yet another gate. From here, run east on top of a mesa that overlooks Boulder Valley Ranch. From the mesa, the trail drops down the steepest part of the run, to a ditch and a wide, roadlike path. Continue on this, first east, then north, and past a little pond, before making a short climb to reach Sage Trail. Take a left to head west, past some ranch structures and back to the trailhead where you started the loop.

MARSHALL MESA

AT BOULDER'S SOUTHERN EDGE, THIS RUN OFFERS TREMENDOUS VIEWS of the Flatirons and the peaks behind them. These trails have been revitalized over the last several years and attract many a mountain biker, which helps buff out the relatively flat route. The lack of vertical and the smooth surface translates to a fast training route or an easy recovery run.

MARSHALL MESA

THE RUN DOWN

START: Marshall Mesa Trailhead

OVERALL DISTANCE: 8.1-mile loop

APPROXIMATE RUNNING TIME: 1.5 hours

DIFFICULTY: Green

ELEVATION GAIN: 861 feet

BEST SEASON TO RUN: Year-round; especially in winter when other trails may be icy

DOG FRIENDLY: Dogs must be on leash at trailheads; under voice and sight command along the trail

PARKING: Free

OTHER USERS: Hikers, mountain bikers, equestrians

CELL PHONE COVERAGE: Yes

MORE INFORMATION: https://bouldercolorado.gov/osmp/marshall-mesa-trailhead

FINDING THE TRAILHEAD

From downtown Boulder, take Broadway/CO 93 south to the stoplight at Eldorado Springs, where you take a left, and then an immediate right, into the free parking area.

RUN DESCRIPTION

From the trailhead, head south (up) on a short climb to where Coal Seam Trail meets Marshall Valley Trail. Stay on Coal Seam to an area that feels

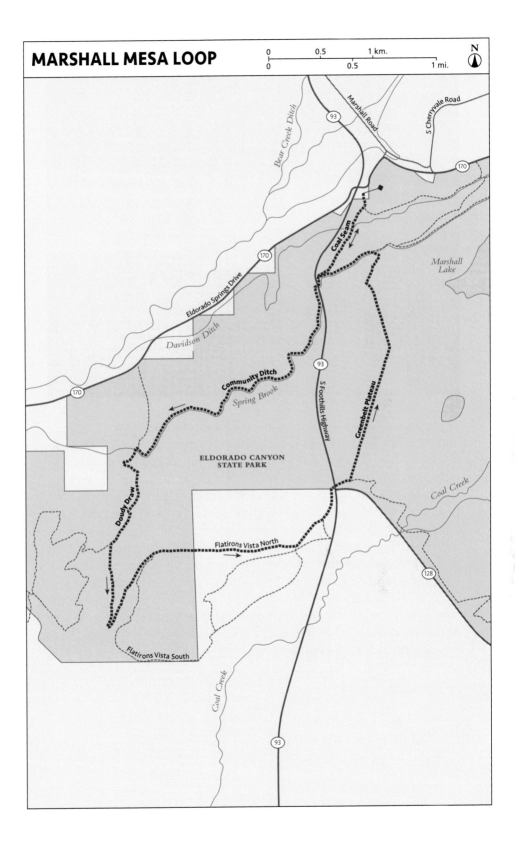

MARSHALL MESA LOOP

0   0.5   1 km.
0   0.5   1 mi.

N

Bear Creek Ditch

93

Marshall Road

S Cherryvale Road

170

Coal Seam

Marshall Lake

170

Eldorado Springs Drive

Davidson Ditch

Community Ditch

Spring Brook

93

S Foothills Highway

Greenbelt Plateau

170

ELDORADO CANYON
STATE PARK

Coal Creek

Dowdy Draw

Flatirons Vista North

128

Flatirons Vista South

Coal Creek

93

Runners enjoy a spring day
on the Marshall Mesa trails.
PHOTO BY TODD STRAKA

like you are running on Moab's slickrock. Coal Seam converges with Community Ditch Trail near an underpass that brings you under CO 93, heading west, with Eldorado Canyon beckoning you as you cruise along the ditch on a flat, fast path. At this point, 2.5 miles in, you meet up with the Doudy Draw Trail, where you take a left, to the south. Climb up from here, passing the Spring Brook Trail on your right (at mile 3.2), and ascending some switchbacks to top out on a mesa, where the North and South Flatirons Vista Trails meet at mile 4.2. Follow the North Flatirons Vista Trail on a graceful descent that takes you to a parking lot, where you meet up with the Greenbelt Connector Trail. Cross over CO 93 to the Greenbelt Plateau Trail at mile 5.7, a wide path that leads north to the edge of the mesa, where the trail turns to the north and great views open to your left. At just over 7 miles, take Community Ditch Trail to Coal Seam Trail for an easy descent back to the trailhead.

HEIL VALLEY RANCH

WAPITI-PONDEROSA LOOP

THE RUN DOWN

START: Heil Valley Ranch Trailhead

OVERALL DISTANCE: 7.9-mile lollipop

APPROXIMATE RUNNING TIME: 100 minutes

DIFFICULTY: Blue

ELEVATION GAIN: 993 feet

BEST SEASON TO RUN: Year-round

DOG FRIENDLY: No dogs allowed

PARKING: Free

OTHER USERS: Hikers, equestrians, mountain bikers

CELL PHONE COVERAGE: Good

MORE INFORMATION: www .bouldercounty.org/os/parks/ pages/heilranch.aspx

FINDING THE TRAILHEAD

Head west on Lefthand Canyon Drive from US 36/North Foothills Highway, which is between Boulder and Lyons. Take your first right on Geer Canyon Drive, which turns to dirt and ends at the trailhead about 1 mile from the canyon. There is a large group shelter at the main trailhead and parking for more than fifty vehicles.

RUN DESCRIPTION

Purchased by Boulder County Parks and Open Space in 1993–1994, these 5,200 acres of sandstone-rich land near Lyons were used for quarry operations, and the quality and quantity of the rock is abundantly clear on the trails, which were built and then reinforced after the 2013 floods. They are presently—and promise to be for many decades to come—built with the meticulous dedication, mostly by Boulder Mountainbike Alliance volunteers, so that they conjure images of Roman or Greek architecture.

From the trailhead and picnic area, the trail climbs a dirt road before you take a left on the Wapiti Trail, heading into a wide meadow, where you begin a series of switchbacks as you ascend into the woods for a steady, gradual singletrack climb of more than 2 miles. Ascend to the junction with the Ponderosa Loop and, being a loop, it doesn't matter if you go clockwise or counter. Until you reach the Ponderosa Loop, the rocky terrain is mostly to the side of the well-groomed trail, but on the Ponderosa Loop you will encounter many a protruding rock. Be sure to take a moment at the overlook, where you'll find two benches. It is a great vantage point to scope out Hall Ranch, and you can even extend this run by taking Picture Rock Trail to Lyons to hitch up to Hall Ranch. Complete the Ponderosa Loop and connect back to Wapiti for a swooping descent back to the start.

HALL RANCH

BITTERBRUSH–NELSON LOOP

THE RUN DOWN

START: Hall Ranch Trailhead

OVERALL DISTANCE: 9.4-mile lollipop

APPROXIMATE RUNNING TIME: 2 hours

DIFFICULTY: Black

ELEVATION GAIN: 1,450 feet

BEST SEASON TO RUN: Year-round

DOG FRIENDLY: No dogs allowed

PARKING: Free

OTHER USERS: Hikers, equestrians, mountain bikers

CELL PHONE COVERAGE: Good

MORE INFORMATION: www .bouldercounty.org/os/parks/ pages/hallranch.aspx

FINDING THE TRAILHEAD

From Lyons, take CO 7/South Saint Vrain Drive west for 1 mile and look for the parking lot on your right. There is plenty of parking, a restroom, and a covered picnic area.

RUN DESCRIPTION

This lollipop loop takes the Bitterbrush Trail to the upper Nelson Loop Trail for a rolling ascent to the elevated meadow at the heart of Hall Ranch, in a mixed ecosystem of grasslands, shrubby hills, and forested areas with pine, ponderosa, and Douglas fir. Beware of rattlesnakes, the only wildlife that pose a threat during the hotter months.

From the upper parking lot follow Bitterbrush Trail up for the first mile, and then enjoy a short drop into a valley. Head up from there, ascending through a meadow, where the trail gets pretty rocky and climbs more dramatically for almost 2 miles before some relief. At 3.7 miles into the run, you'll reach the 2.3-mile Nelson Loop. Travel in either direction, enjoying more climbing on a pedestrian-only trail, and some awesome views, before you drop back to reconnect to Bitterbrush Trail and a cruiser descent to the parking lot.

BOULDER URBAN TRAIL

BOULDER URBAN TRAIL

THE RUN DOWN

START: Pearl Street Mall

OVERALL DISTANCE: 6.4 miles

APPROXIMATE RUNNING TIME: 1 hour

DIFFICULTY: Green

ELEVATION GAIN: 548 feet

BEST SEASON TO RUN: Year-round

DOG FRIENDLY: Leashed dogs permitted

PARKING: Available in town, metered or in parking garages

OTHER USERS: Walkers and others typical for an urban setting

CELL PHONE COVERAGE: Excellent

MORE INFORMATION: https://bouldercolorado.gov/parks-rec/parks-recreation-pearl-street-mall

FINDING THE TRAILHEAD

This run begins at the west end of the Pearl Street Mall in downtown Boulder.

RUN DESCRIPTION

This fun "city trail" tour of Boulder takes you through many of its neighborhoods for some urban adventure and on slightly hidden trails. Start with what may be tourist, stroller, and texting-teen dodging as you run east on the Pearl Street Mall and through the grounds of the Boulder County Courthouse. Pass the Boulder Theater on 14th Street and keep heading north. Take a right on Pine Street and run past the "Mork and Mindy" house. Take a left on 19th Street to Bluff Street, where you follow a slightly hidden trail that leads to a sharp left onto a tunnel-like trail, which takes you to Sunset Boulevard's terminus. Follow Sunset to High Street, and then take a right on a trail that swoops above Casey Middle School and leads down to North Street.

Take North Street west to 13th Street, where you take a left. Run through the parking structure to make your way to Broadway. Use the pedestrian crossing to keep going west, following Maxwell Avenue to 9th Street, where you can cross over and use alleys to take you west, across 4th Street, to the grounds of the old sanitarium and the base of Mount Sanitas. Go left and down to the trailhead when you hit Sanitas Valley. Cross over Sunshine Canyon Drive to Green Rock Drive and, at its end, look for a small path to your left. This will lead you along a stream and to west Pearl Street, where you take a right to the bike path that passes under Canyon Boulevard and over Boulder Creek. Take a left at Eben G. Fine Park and run across Arapahoe Avenue to the alley, heading to a trail at the base of Flagstaff. Bear left at the junction on a short rocky trail to Marshall Street, where you head up to your right.

Marshall bends into Pleasant Street. Take your first right onto Jay Street, and then an immediate left on to Hopgood. Pass 6th Street to an alley that leads to Dean Place and 7th Street, where you take a right on Pleasant to run by Columbia Cemetery. Go across 9th Street, through student housing on University Hill, and then onto the University of Colorado campus. Take a left at the Old Main building, taking a walkway over a bridge, and then the next right to cross over University Avenue. Go straight through to a small walkway that runs to your left, down stairs, and behind the Boulder High School stadium before linking up with the bike path that leads down across the Boulder Creek, and under Arapahoe and Broadway, to take you back to where you started at Pearl.

DOUDY DRAW

DOUDY DRAW

THE RUN DOWN

START: Doudy Draw trailhead parking lot; elevation 5,665 feet

OVERALL DISTANCE: 5.1-mile lollipop

APPROXIMATE RUNNING TIME: 1 hour

DIFFICULTY: Blue

ELEVATION GAIN: 547 feet

BEST SEASON TO RUN: Year-round

DOG FRIENDLY: Boulder rules of voice-and sight-command apply; a leash is required near the trailhead. Dogs are not permitted on Spring Brook Loop South or Goshawk Ridge Trail, and must be on leash on Spring Brook North and seasonally on the upper section of Doudy Draw, south of Community Ditch and west of Flatirons Vista, due to bear activity.

PARKING: A fee is levied for non-Boulder County residents; an annual pass is also an option

OTHER USERS: Hikers, equestrians, mountain bikes

CELL PHONE COVERAGE: Good

MORE INFORMATION: https://bouldercolorado.gov/osmp/doudy-draw-trailhead

FINDING THE TRAILHEAD

The trailhead is located south of downtown Boulder and 1.8 miles west of CO 93 on Eldorado Springs Drive (CO 170). Restrooms are a third of a mile south of the trailhead on Doudy Draw Trail.

RUN DESCRIPTION

There are many options for extending this run, or making it more or less challenging. From the trailhead, the trail is a groomed gravel path for half-a-mile of gentle climbing, to where it intersects with the Community Ditch, which runs east–west and connects to Marshall Mesa through an underpass—if you were to take a left on it. Don't. Stay straight (south), and follow Doudy Draw Trail for 1.7 miles to the junction with the Spring Brook Loop Trail, which heads west. The loop begins soon thereafter, and circles around on the twisty and wooded Spring Brook Loop North trail, and then the Spring Brook Loop South Trail, before connecting back to Doudy Draw for your return. The footing is normally dry and rocky, but not very technical. Watch for bike traffic, and avoid running this on windy days, as it is quite open and exposed.

OPTION: MARSHALL MESA CONNECTION

Make the same start as for Doudy Draw, but take a left when you reach the Community Ditch. The "trail" is essentially a dirt road along an irrigation canal. Follow the ditch-side path east for about 1.75 miles, and through an underpass under CO 93. You can stay on the Community Ditch Trail for almost 2 miles, heading east with almost no altitude change. Bear left at the junction with Cowdrey Draw Trail and, shortly thereafter, make another left, to the northwest, onto Mesa Valley Trail. This connects with the Marshall Mesa Trail, which heads west to reconnect with the Community Ditch Trail and brings you back to Doudy Draw to return to the parking area.

As an alternative, after taking the underpass on the Community Ditch Trail, you can take the Greenbelt Plateau Trail, climbing to the south and paralleling CO 93 to link up with the High Plains Trail to the east, or the Flatirons Vista Trail to the west, which crosses over the highway for a long loop back to Doudy Draw.

DENVER RUNS

NORTH TABLE MOUNTAIN LOOP

LOCATED ON THE OUTSKIRTS OF THE CITIES OF GOLDEN AND ARVADA, North Table Mountain Park—and the loop that encircles the outer perimeter of the park—offers runners a moderate run on smooth singletrack. Providing excellent views to the east, as well as wildlife encounters with coyotes, mule deer, red-tailed hawks, and other animals, the North Table Mountain Loop is a unique run along the Front Range.

NORTH TABLE MOUNTAIN LOOP

THE RUN DOWN

START: North Table Mountain trailhead; elevation 6,014 feet

OVERALL DISTANCE: 7.5 miles round-trip

APPROXIMATE RUNNING TIME: 1 to 1.5 hours

DIFFICULTY: Green to Blue

ELEVATION GAIN: 1,424 feet

BEST SEASON TO RUN: Year-round, although fall through spring are best; summer can be hot

DOG FRIENDLY: Dogs must be on leash at all times

PARKING: Free

OTHER USERS: Hikers, equestrians, mountain bikers

CELL PHONE COVERAGE: Good

MORE INFORMATION: http://jeffco.us/parks/

FINDING THE TRAILHEAD

The North Table Mountain trailhead is located just north of the city of Golden. Take CO 93 north from Golden and turn right (east) immediately after passing Pine Ridge Road. Follow the sign to the large parking lot. The trail starts on the north end of the parking lot.

RUN DESCRIPTION

This loop can be run either clockwise or counterclockwise; the counterclockwise direction is described here. From the parking lot, the trail follows the very steep dirt service road to the top of the mesa. This is the steepest part of the entire run, and it only lasts for 0.6 mile. Once on top of the mesa, the North Table loop turns right (south) and continues on the dirt service road past an old quarry and two climber access trails.

At the 1.0-mile mark, the North Table loop branches off from the dirt service road and heads east on singletrack, as you gently descend along a small wash off the mesa and through a small canyon before continuing east below the cliffs of the mesa. Continue running east as the trail rolls along just below the mesa cliffs, providing excellent views down into Clear Creek, the city of Golden, and east into Denver.

Soon the trail turns and begins traversing another small canyon, where a neighborhood connector trail joins in at mile 2.6. Continue on the main trail east, crossing a small seasonal stream before gently climbing to meet up with the Cottonwood Canyon trail (mile 2.8).

Continue east on the North Table loop as the trail begins to curve around to the east side of the mesa, at which point it quickly descends through a couple of switchbacks before meeting up with the Lithic Trail (mile 3.7). This is the lowest point in the loop.

Continue on the North Table loop heading north, as you gently climb on singletrack, traversing across another small canyon while enjoying unique views to the east of Denver, Arvada, and beyond. The trail continues to hug the edge of the mesa cliffs on rolling singletrack as it passes the turnoff for the Mesa Top Trail (mile 4.1).

Soon the trail turns west and quickly descends to another dirt service road (mile 5.4). Turn left (west) and run up and along the service road as it briefly climbs and then descends again on the western side of the mesa. The North Table loop stays on this dirt service road past the turnoff for the Table Rock Trail shortcut (mile 5.6) before beginning to climb again, at which point the North Table loop leaves the dirt service road and turns back into singletrack (mile 6.4).

Turn onto the singletrack and follow as it rolls through open prairie along the northwestern edge of the mesa before turning south and returning to the parking lot and the start (mile 7.5). The trails within the North Table Mountain Park are multiuse, so mountain bikes and horses may be encountered. Please be respectful of other trail users.

GOLDEN GATE CANYON LOOP

THIS LOOP IS LOCATED WITHIN GOLDEN GATE CANYON STATE PARK, providing excellent singletrack that runs through open meadows and aspen and pine forests. With several stream crossings, a solid climb, and a fun and fast descent, this loop run follows the Mountain Lion Trail as it circles Windy Peak.

GOLDEN GATE CANYON LOOP

THE RUN DOWN

START: Mountain Lion Trailhead in the Nott Creek parking lot; elevation 7,700 feet

OVERALL DISTANCE: 7 miles round-trip

APPROXIMATE RUNNING TIME: 1 to 1.5 hours

DIFFICULTY: Blue

ELEVATION GAIN: 1,690 feet

BEST SEASON TO RUN: Spring through fall; spring can be muddy and the stream crossings can have high water

DOG FRIENDLY: Dogs must be on leash at all times

PARKING: An entrance fee is charged

OTHER USERS: Hikers, equestrians, mountain bikers

CELL PHONE COVERAGE: Bad

MORE INFORMATION: www .parks.state.co.us/parks/ goldengatecanyon/pages/ goldengatestatepark.aspx

FINDING THE TRAILHEAD

The Mountain Lion Trail starts and ends at the Nott Creek parking lot. From the city of Golden, take CO 93 north 1 mile to Golden Gate

Canyon Road. Turn left (west) and follow the road 13 miles to the park entrance. From the park entrance, turn right (east) onto Drew Hill Road and follow it 3.4 miles to the turnoff for the Nott Creek parking lot. Turn left (north) onto the dirt road and follow it 0.2 mile to the parking area. The Mountain Lion Trail starts from the north side of the parking area. The park requires a day pass, which can be purchased at the visitor center.

RUN DESCRIPTION

This loop can be run either clockwise or counterclockwise; the counterclockwise direction is described here. From the parking area, the Mountain Lion Trail begins with a very short climb that quickly turns into rolling two-track trail traveling through open meadows. After a fun mile that provides wonderful views to the east, the trail descends and curves north, dropping you into the small canyon formed by Deer Creek (mile 1.4).

Once in the canyon, the trail travels through dispersed aspen and pine forests as it gently climbs over rocky terrain along the edge of Deer Creek. The trail continues to follow Deer Creek, crossing the creek eleven times before eventually moving away from the creek at mile 3.1. From here, the trail steeply climbs through a dense pine forest, around several switchbacks, before reaching a small saddle below Windy Peak (mile 3.7).

From the saddle, the trail quickly descends through some switchbacks into beautiful Forgotten Valley. Continue on the Mountain Lion Trail, passing the turnoff for the Buffalo Trail (mile 4.5) on your right (west). The Mountain Lion Trail passes a small pond before crossing over a small stream and gently climbing again toward the southeast.

After a short climb, the trail again descends. Pass the junction with the City Lights Ridge Trail (mile 5.2) and the Burro Trail (mile 5.4). Stay on the Mountain Lion Trail as it follows the ridge over three very small climbs before quickly dropping you back down to the Nott Creek dirt road and the parking area.

The trails within the Golden Gate Canyon State Park are multiuse, so mountain bikes and horses may be encountered—please be respectful of other trail users.

GREEN MOUNTAIN LOOP

LOCATED IN THE WILLIAM F. HAYDEN PARK ON GREEN MOUNTAIN, this loop run follows a series of multiuse trails around Green Mountain, offering unique views of the Denver metropolitan area to the east as well as the high mountain peaks to the west.

GREEN MOUNTAIN LOOP

THE RUN DOWN

START: The trailhead at West Alameda Parkway and West Florida Drive; elevation: 6,100 feet

OVERALL DISTANCE: 6.5-mile loop

APPROXIMATE RUNNING TIME: 45 minutes to 1.5 hours

DIFFICULTY: Green to Blue

ELEVATION GAIN: 1,180 feet

BEST SEASON TO RUN: Year-round; summer can be hot as

there is no shade, and winter can be warm and dry

DOG FRIENDLY: Dogs must be on leash at all times

PARKING: Free

OTHER USERS: Hikers, equestrians, mountain bikers

CELL PHONE COVERAGE: Good

MORE INFORMATION: www .lakewood.org/Community_ Resources/Parks,_Forestry_ and_Open_Space/

FINDING THE TRAILHEAD

The William F. Hayden Park on Green Mountain is located on the outskirts of the city of Lakewood. There are multiple trailheads and access points; the run described here begins on the southeast side of the park at the intersection of West Alameda Parkway and West Florida Drive. Take CO 470 (C-470) south from I-70 to the West Alameda Parkway exit. Upon exiting, turn left (east) and follow West Alameda Parkway underneath C-470 as it traverses around the south side of Green Mountain to the intersection with West Florida Drive. The parking area and trail-head are located across from West Florida Drive.

RUN DESCRIPTION

This loop can be run either clockwise or counterclockwise; the clockwise direction is described here. From the parking lot, begin by following the Green Mountain Trail west as it rolls along the southern edge of Green Mountain. After a short bit, the trail crosses the Hayden Trail (mile 0.4) as it continues to roll west through open grassland, providing exceptional views of the Dakota Hogback extending north-south along the foothills.

At mile 1.0, the Green Mountain Trail crosses the Rooney Valley Trail before dropping down and crossing a service road near West Alameda Parkway. Continue past the service road as the trail now begins to head north, slowly curving away from West Alameda Parkway and gently climbing up along the western slopes of Green Mountain.

At mile 2.6, the Green Mountain Trail again crosses the Rooney Valley Trail on the right (east); continue running due north on rolling singletrack before the trail merges with a service road near C-470 (mile 3.4). At this point the loop turns onto the service road and begins the longest climb of the run, as you make your way to the top of Green Mountain, passing the turnoff for the Box O' Rox Trail on the left (north) at mile 3.6. From the top of Green Mountain, excellent views in all directions can be had.

After climbing to the top of Green Mountain, the service road makes a sharp turn to the south (mile 4.4) before beginning a fun descent back toward the parking area. At mile 5.2 the loop passes the Hayden Trail on the right (south) before reaching the prominent radio tower located on the south side of Green Mountain. At the radio tower follow the service road to the right (south) as it heads down back toward West Alameda Parkway and the parking area just 1 mile beyond.

The trails within William F. Hayden Park are multiuse, so mountain bikes and horses may be encountered. Please be respectful of other trail users.

MOUNT FALCON

THIS RUN INVOLVES A SOLID CLIMB UP TO THE TOP OF MOUNT FALCON with a small lollipop loop around an open meadow, providing rewarding views and panoramas of the Mount Evans Wilderness to the west, Red Rocks Park to the north, and the Denver cityscape to the east.

MOUNT FALCON

THE RUN DOWN

START: Mount Falcon East trailhead; elevation 6,000 feet

OVERALL DISTANCE: 8.5-mile lollipop

APPROXIMATE RUNNING TIME: 1 to 2 hours

DIFFICULTY: Black

ELEVATION GAIN: 1,973 feet

BEST SEASON TO RUN: Year-round; summer can be hot and snow may be present in winter

DOG FRIENDLY: Dogs must be on leash at all times

PARKING: Free

OTHER USERS: Hikers, equestrians, mountain bikers

CELL PHONE COVERAGE: Average

MORE INFORMATION: http://jeffco.us/parks/

FINDING THE TRAILHEAD

Mount Falcon Park is located just outside of the town of Morrison. From downtown Morrison, continue west on Bear Creek Avenue/Morrison Road (the main street), turning left (south) onto CO 8 right after passing through downtown. Continue on CO 8 for 0.8 mile to Forest Avenue. Turn right (west) onto Forest Avenue, and then right again on Vine Street. Follow Vine Street to the end of the road and the large parking area.

RUN DESCRIPTION

This run provides a strenuous workout that is used by many local runners as a training ground for bigger adventures in the high mountains. From the parking area, the run starts on the multiuse Castle Trail, but quickly turns off onto the hiker-only Turkey Trot Trail. Continue up the Turkey Trot Trail as it initially climbs a very steep section through a series of switchbacks before mellowing out a touch.

After the first mile, the trail curves around to the north side of Mount Falcon and eases up to become an enjoyable run on a mellow grade, with interesting views of Red Rocks Park and Bear Creek just to the north.

At mile 1.5 the trail turns east again, up a final switchback, before merging back with the Castle Trail (mile 1.7). Turn right on the Castle Trail and continue climbing as the trail snakes its way along the southeastern slopes of Mount Falcon. After close to a mile more of climbing the somewhat rocky trail, the run enters a brief section of shade as it switchbacks up the final portion of the trail before reaching a small shelter (mile 3.0).

At the shelter, the singletrack trail ends and the Castle Trail turns into a gravel service road; continue west on the gravel service road, passing the turnoff for Walker's Dream Trail (on the right) and the Two-Dog Trail (on the left). The gravel service road continues west as it rolls along the ridge before reaching the old historic Walker Home ruins (mile 3.4). At the ruins, turn left (south) onto the Meadow Trail, which skirts around the eastern and southern portions of a large open meadow, often filled with wildflowers in the spring and summer.

At mile 3.7 the Meadow Trail meets up with the Old Ute Trail and the Parmalee Trail; continue on the Meadow Trail as it continues to encircle the open meadow. Right after passing the Parmalee Trail, turn off onto the Tower Trail for the final 0.5-mile climb to the top of Mount Falcon (7,851 feet). At the top of Mount Falcon, climb up to the viewing platform on the top of the old fire watch tower (mile 4.25).

From the top of Mount Falcon, run down the opposite side that you ascended, toward the Eagle Eye shelter, which provides outstanding views of the high peaks to the west. Continue down the trail, which turns back into a gravel service road as you run along the western edge of the open meadow before connecting back up with the Castle Trail (mile 4.5). Turn right (east) back onto the Castle Trail and follow it as it rolls back down toward the Walker Home ruins.

From the Walker Home ruins, retrace the run back down the Castle Trail and the Turkey Trot Trail to the parking area about 2,000 feet below.

The trails within Mount Falcon Park are multiuse, so mountain bikes and horses may be encountered. Please be respectful of other trail users.

CHERRY CREEK STATE PARK LOOP

THIS IS A NICE LOOP RUN AROUND CHERRY CREEK RESERVOIR in Cherry Creek State Park, offering runners a natural prairie environment of gentle, rolling hills. With open grasslands, cottonwood trees, and marshes this loop run is great for speed work or mellower recovery runs.

CHERRY CREEK STATE PARK LOOP

THE RUN DOWN

START: West entrance parking area; elevation 5,600 feet

APPROXIMATE RUNNING TIME: 1 to 1.5 hours

OVERALL DISTANCE: 8.7-mile loop

DIFFICULTY: Green

ELEVATION GAIN: 446 feet

BEST SEASON TO RUN: Year-round; summer can be hot and snow may be present in winter

DOG FRIENDLY: Dogs must be on leash at all times

PARKING: An entrance fee is charged

OTHER USERS: Hikers, mountain bikers

CELL PHONE COVERAGE: Good

MORE INFORMATION: www.parks.state.co.us/ Parks/CherryCreek/Pages/ CherryCreekHome.aspx

FINDING THE TRAILHEAD

The run starts and ends at the large parking area just inside the park's west entrance. From I-25 heading south from downtown Denver, take the I-225 exit and follow I-225 east to South Yosemite Street. Turn south onto South Yosemite Street and continue to East Union Avenue. Turn left (east) onto East Union Avenue and follow it around to the west entrance, just south of the junction of East Union Avenue and South

Dayton Street. The large parking area is just inside the park entrance on the left, near the west boat ramp.

RUN DESCRIPTION

This loop run can be done either clockwise or counterclockwise; the counterclockwise direction is described here. Encircling the entire Cherry Creek Reservoir, this loop run provides runners with wonderful opportunities to see bald eagles, red-tailed hawks, and great horned owls perched in the surrounding cottonwoods, as well as other waterfowl and shorebirds, along with mule deer, coyotes, and prairie species.

Beginning from the large parking area near the west entrance of the park, the run begins by following the Cherry Creek Trail, a paved trail that heads south out of the parking area, crosses the park entrance road, and quickly turns southeast. After 0.4 mile the trail recrosses the park road and meanders along the southeast shore of the reservoir, with tall cottonwoods on one side and open prairie on the other. Continue running along the Cherry Creek Trail as you pass several picnic areas until you reach the turnoff for the Pipeline Trail (mile 2.0).

Turn left (east) onto the Pipeline Trail and follow it east across the expansive marsh and riparian habitat as you cross Cherry Creek. Shortly after crossing Cherry Creek, the Pipeline Trail ends at the Parker Road Trail; turn left (north) and continue running on the Parker Road Trail along the edge of a stand of some large cottonwoods before reaching the shores of the reservoir once again.

At mile 3.2 there is a junction. Take the right junction and turn away from the reservoir, cross the road, and begin a small climb. Near the 3.6-mile mark the Parker Road Trail turns north and parallels South Parker Road; continue running on the Parker Road Trail through open prairie as the trail winds along between South Parker Road and the internal park roads.

At mile 4.25 the trail crosses East Lehigh Avenue as it continues to parallel South Parker Road on the right, with expansive rolling grasslands on the left.

After another rolling mile, the trail crosses the Dam Road (mile 5.3) and merges back onto the Cherry Creek Trail before beginning a mellow, rolling descent. This rolling descent continues for 1 mile (mile 6.4) before the trail begins to gently climb once again, as it continues west and eventually southwest around the reservoir's dam.

At mile 8.2 the Cherry Creek Trail arrives at the junction of East Union Avenue and the Dam Road, which is where the west park entrance is located. Cross the Dam Road and continue east past the park entrance back to your original starting point at the large parking area just inside the park.

The trails within Cherry Creek State Park are multiuse, so mountain bikes and horses may be encountered. Please be respectful of other trail users.

WHITE RANCH PARK

WHITE RANCH IS A LARGE PARK WITH A LOT OF GREAT TRAILS. Rising in the foothills just west of Arvada, White Ranch is home to abundant wildlife, a mix of terrain, and over 20 miles of trails. Most trails involve some climbing, but the effort is well worth it as the park offers spectacular views, large open meadows, and forested, rolling trails.

The gate at White Ranch maintains the park's historic character.
PHOTO BY PETER N. JONES

LONGHORN TO SHORTHORN LOOP

This is a fun loop with decent climbs, offering great views to the east and a fun section through rolling, forested terrain. Mule deer are often seen on this run, and in the spring wildflowers are often abundant on the surrounding slopes.

THE RUN DOWN

START: White Ranch East Trailhead

OVERALL DISTANCE: 6-mile lollipop

APPROXIMATE RUNNING TIME: 1 to 1.5 hours

DIFFICULTY: Blue

ELEVATION GAIN: 1,235 feet

BEST SEASON TO RUN: Year-round, although summer can be hot and winter can be snowy

DOG FRIENDLY: Dogs must be on leash at all times

PARKING: Free

OTHER USERS: Hikers, mountain bikers, equestrians

CELL PHONE COVERAGE: Average

MORE INFORMATION: http://jeffco.us/open-space/parks/white-ranch-park/

FINDING THE TRAILHEAD

The White Ranch East Trailhead is located on the eastern side of the park, right off Glencoe Valley Road. Take CO 93 north from Golden for 1.7 miles to West 56th Avenue. Turn left onto West 56th Avenue, also known as Pine Ridge Road, and follow it about 1 mile to the parking lot located at the base of the foothills.

RUN DESCRIPTION

From the parking area, start on the Belcher Hill Trail and go through the two gates as the trail heads north through a private neighborhood. After the second gate, the trail runs through some rocky and sandy terrain along the bottom of Van Bibber Creek before climbing out of the creek valley

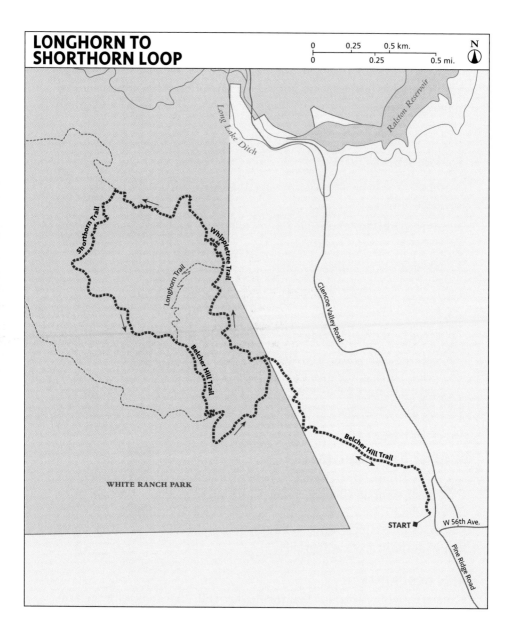

LONGHORN TO
SHORTHORN LOOP

0   0.25   0.5 km.

0   0.25   0.5 mi.

N

Ralston Reservoir

Long Lake Ditch

Shorthorn Trail

Whippletree Trail

Longhorn Trail

Belcher Hill Trail

Glencoe Valley Road

Belcher Hill Trail

WHITE RANCH PARK

START

W 56th Ave.

Pine Ridge Road

on the western side. At mile 0.6 the trail crosses Van Bibber Creek again, before slowly climbing north along the lower flanks of the foothills. At mile 1.1, just beyond a sharp switchback, the Whippletree Trail is encountered on your right; turn onto the Whippletree Trail and follow it as it rolls north.

As the trail begins to descend into a gully, the Whippletree Trail ends and the Longhorn Trail is reached. Continue north on the Longhorn Trail as it descends into the bottom of the ravine before beginning a steep climb up the adjacent slope.

After a fair bit of climbing, the Shorthorn Trail is encountered on the left at mile 2.6. Turn onto the Shorthorn Trail as it heads back south and begins to roll through the mixed forest. After some fun rolling terrain, the Shorthorn Trail ends when it meets back up with the Longhorn Trail at mile 3.8.

After a fun and fast descent, the Longhorn Trail dumps you out back onto the Belcher Hill Trail; turn left and continue running down the Belcher Hill Trail all the way back to the trailhead to complete the loop.

LONGHORN TO BELCHER HILL LOOP

This loop run is a continuation of the Longhorn to Shorthorn Loop, but with more climbing and a loop around the large open meadow at the top of the park. With stiff climbs and steep descents, this run offers everything to get the heart pounding and the legs working.

THE RUN DOWN

START: White Ranch East Trailhead

OVERALL DISTANCE: 7.5-mile lollipop

APPROXIMATE RUNNING TIME: 1 to 2 hours

DIFFICULTY: Black

ELEVATION GAIN: 1,635 feet

BEST SEASON TO RUN: Year-round, although summer can be hot and winter can be snowy

DOG FRIENDLY: Dogs must be on leash at all times

PARKING: Free

OTHER USERS: Hikers, mountain bikers, equestrians

CELL PHONE COVERAGE: Average

MORE INFORMATION: http:// jeffco.us/open-space/parks/ white-ranch-park/

FINDING THE TRAILHEAD

The White Ranch East Trailhead is located on the eastern side of the park, right off Glencoe Valley Road. Take CO 93 north from Golden for 1.7 miles to West 56th Avenue. Turn left onto West 56th Avenue, also known as Pine Ridge Road, and follow it about 1 mile to the parking lot located at the base of the foothills.

RUN DESCRIPTION

This loop is a continuation of Longhorn to Shorthorn Loop, finishing the climb up Longhorn to the big meadow at the top before the long and steep descent back down.

LONGHORN TO BELCHER HILL LOOP

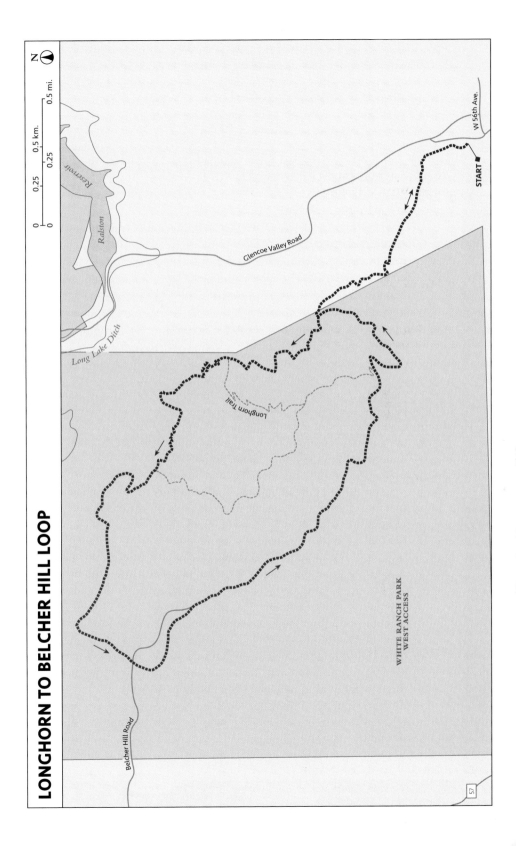

INJURY PREVENTION

FORTUNATELY, TRAIL RUNNERS TEND TO BE A RELATIVELY HEALTHY lot, and running on soft surfaces reduces the likelihood of certain types of injury. Then again, sometimes trail running is indeed a contact sport. Unlike the typical and seemingly mundane repetitive stress injuries suffered by road runners, trail runners are known to adorn themselves with surface lacerations that are much more fascinating than tendonitis, shin splints, or chondromalacia, which are not visible to the naked eye. Yet a mishap with the trail, a tree, rocks, a cliff, or some ice is just as likely to result in a subtle overuse problem as it is in a more dramatic flesh wound. Trail runners are not invincible. They do, from time to time, suffer injuries, and even fall prey to the same overuse problems that plague road runners.

Severe acute injuries are likely to require medical attention. In contrast, common trail running trauma—strained joints from sudden efforts to avoid falling, and abrasions and bruising from falls that were not avoided—are usually remedied by rest and ice. When possible, end a trail run near a cool body of water, such as a stream, river, or mountain pond, which can be used for an invigorating and therapeutic soak. Elevating your legs after a hard effort also helps to flush the blood from battered muscle tissue and reduce inflammation. Compression socks or calf sleeves or tights also help with pushing blood out of your recovering lower leg muscles.

Twisted or rolled ankles are dreaded by all trail runners. A momentary lapse of concentration, a misstep, a shaded divot, some slippery mud or ice, or simple lack of coordination is all it takes to cause an ankle to twist or roll. Depending on the severity, a twisted or rolled ankle can result in minor muscle tears, swelling, tendon and ligament damage, or even broken bones. If the twist or roll results in substantial pain and swelling, it is a good idea to consult with a medical professional to determine the seriousness of the injury.

The best treatment for ankle problems is to avoid them by strengthening the muscles that support the ankle and working on flexibility of the area through stretching. If you are vulnerable to ankle twists or rolls, wear trail shoes with higher ankle collars, or wrap or tape your ankles for additional support. Consult with a trainer, physical therapist, or other health care professional to learn proper ankle-taping techniques.

Ligaments work to join bones together. Certain knee ligaments, known by their three-letter abbreviations, have become infamous because of a few other three-letter abbreviations including NFL, NBA, NHL, etc. The ACL (anterior cruciate ligament) and the PCL (posterior cruciate ligament) are found within the knee joint and prevent the femur from sliding too much on the tibia. Trail runners are most prone to a rupture of the ACL when a foot planted on uneven ground forces the leg to rotate excessively at the knee. Stretching and strengthening the quadriceps and hamstrings will help to keep the damage to a minimum.

Overuse injuries are caused from any one of a number or a combination of various factors, including incorrect running form, running in shoes that have lost their cushioning and support, and long, jarring descents on rocky, compacted, or other hard surfaces, especially when the leg muscles are already fatigued so they do not absorb the impact as readily.

Muscle strain is a type of overuse injury caused by overstretching muscle fiber, and can range from minor microtears to more severe tears or ruptures in deeper muscle tissue. Minor strains manifest themselves through pain and post-trauma stiffness. Depending on the severity of a strain, treatment can include anything from prerun warm-ups and stretching and post-run ice applications, to massage, to medical treatment and rehabilitation.

Trail runners should be aware of the risk of poking an eye, breaking a bone, being lacerated or punctured, or otherwise being harmed in a mishap on the trail. Although the medical response and emergency handling of such calamities is beyond the scope of this book, it is strongly advised that you read up or receive training on wilderness first aid and in-the-field medical care and CPR before venturing out to run the trails.

Horses can be found on the lower section of White Ranch.
PHOTO BY PETER N. JONES

Follow the run description for the Longhorn to Shorthorn Loop, but at the Longhorn/Shorthorn junction (mile 2.6), instead of turning onto the Shorthorn Trail, continue climbing up the Longhorn Trail. From the junction, the Longhorn Trail crosses a small seasonal stream as it switchbacks through another gulch, before beginning a short but steep climb. At mile 3.1 the Maverick Trail branches off to the left; continue on the Longhorn Trail as you reach the eastern side of the large meadow. Near mile 3.4 the Longhorn Trail begins to head slightly north as it circles around the northern and western sides of the small hill, offering up unique views to the north of valleys and red rock formations.

At mile 3.8 the Longhorn Trail ends at the upper parking lot in the center of the large meadow. Cross the parking lot and follow the Sawmill Trail as it rolls along the western side of the meadow, offering spectacular views east down onto the plains and the city of Denver. After a short bit of rolling terrain, the Sawmill Trail ends (mile 4.5) and turns into the Belcher Hill Trail; this is the highest point of the run.

From the high point the run follows the Belcher Hill Trail as it descends steeply back down toward the plains, over rocky and somewhat technical terrain. This section of the loop is a blast to bomb down, but remember to keep a little bit of energy for the final section back to the car, as this descent is known to destroy runners' quads more often than not.

MOUNT GALBRAITH PARK

MOUNT GALBRAITH IS A SMALL PARK, but what it lacks in size it makes up for in views. Consisting of a steep climb and a loop around the summit, this run offers unique views into Clear Creek Canyon to the south and west, and into Golden and west Denver to the east.

MOUNT GALBRAITH LOOP

This is a challenging run, but well worth the effort. Consisting of a short lollipop course, the run climbs up to the top of Mount Galbraith before circling around the summit on a fun, rolling trail that provides vistas and overlooks in all directions.

THE RUN DOWN

START: Cedar Gulch Trailhead

OVERALL DISTANCE: 4.2-mile lollipop

APPROXIMATE RUNNING TIME: 35 minutes to 1 hour

DIFFICULTY: Blue

ELEVATION GAIN: 1,023 feet

BEST SEASON TO RUN: Year-round, although summer can be hot

DOG FRIENDLY: Dogs must be on leash at all times

PARKING: Free

OTHER USERS: Hikers

CELL PHONE COVERAGE: Average

MORE INFORMATION: http://jeffco.us/open-space/parks/mount-galbraith-park/

FINDING THE TRAILHEAD

The Cedar Gulch Trailhead is located directly off Golden Gate Canyon Road just outside Golden. From CO 93 on the north side of Golden, turn left onto Golden Gate Canyon Road. Follow Golden Gate Canyon Road for 1.5 miles to the parking area and trailhead, located on the left.

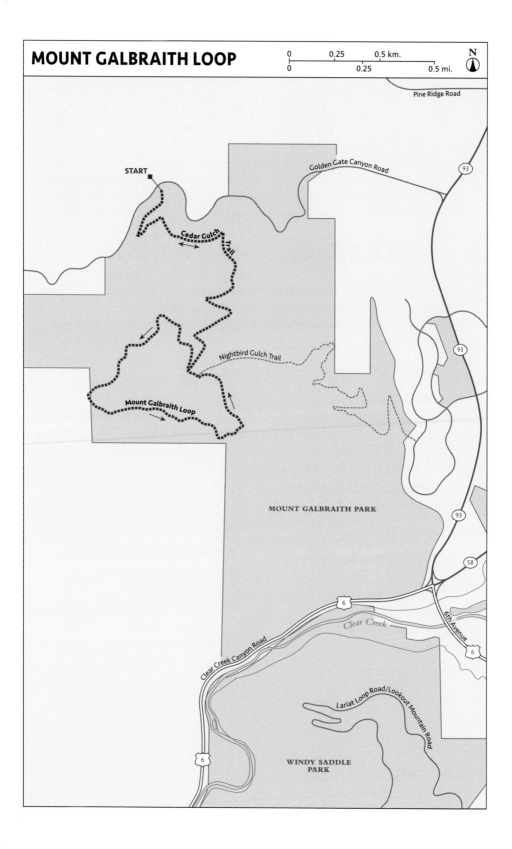

MOUNT GALBRAITH LOOP

0   0.25   0.5 km.

0   0.25   0.5 mi.

N

Pine Ridge Road

Golden Gate Canyon Road

93

START

Cedar Gulch Trail

Nightbird Gulch Trail

93

Mount Galbraith Loop

MOUNT GALBRAITH PARK

93

58

6

Clear Creek

6th Avenue

6

Clear Creek Canyon Road

Lariat Loop Road/Lookout Mountain Road

6

WINDY SADDLE PARK

The route at Mount Galbraith winds and rolls on the upper loop.
PHOTO BY PETER N. JONES

RUN DESCRIPTION

This is a short but hard run. From the trailhead, follow the Cedar Gulch Trail as it immediately begins to climb up the northern side of Mount Galbraith. The trail switchbacks up through mixed forest and open grasses, heading first west and then east. After 1.2 miles of climbing the Cedar Gulch Trail ends and the Mount Galbraith Loop begins. Turn right (west) onto the Mount Galbraith Loop and immediately begin a fast but short descent before climbing again as you loop around in a counterclockwise direction. At mile 2.1 you reach the highest point on the loop, and from here back to the trailhead it is all downhill.

At mile 2.9 you will pass the Nightbird Gulch Trail on your right, and then at mile 3.0 you will reach the Cedar Gulch Trail again, completing the loop. Turn right (north) onto the Cedar Gulch Trail, and bomb it back down to the trailhead to complete the lollipop run for a total of 4.2 miles.

SUMMER WEATHER HAZARDS

SINCE YOU CAN ENCOUNTER ANY NUMBER OF ELEMENTS, surprises, and hazards on the trail, it's important to be prepared. Although some dangers are inherent in the sport, planning ahead and being cautious and aware of your surroundings at all times greatly enhances the trail running experience.

Sunburn: Sunburn can range from mild, if you are prepared enough to use sunblock and to reapply the product as long as exposure continues, to severe, resulting in blisters, fever, and headaches. To treat sunburn, take a shower using soap to remove oils that may block pores and prevent the body from cooling naturally. If blisters occur, apply dry, sterile dressings and seek medical attention. Sunscreen with a high SPF number is an essential addition to every trail runner's fanny pack. A type billed as a "performance" sunscreen is best, since breathability is important to an athlete.

Heat Cramps, Heat Exhaustion, and Heatstroke: The symptoms of heat cramps are painful spasms, usually in the leg and abdominal muscles, often coupled with heavy sweating. To relieve a spasm, apply firm pressure or gently massage the cramping muscles. Sip water unless drinking causes nausea; in that case, cease drinking.

Symptoms of heat exhaustion include heavy sweating, weakness, fainting, weakened pulse, and cold, pale, clammy skin. It is possible for the victim to have a normal temperature. A heat exhaustion victim should be taken to a cool place to lie down, clothing should be loosened, and cool, wet cloths should be applied. Placing ice cubes or plastic bags filled with cold water in the armpits and the crotch also prove beneficial in bringing down the victim's temperature. Be careful, however, to make sure the ice is removed from time to time to prevent frostbite (especially in the crotch). If vomiting occurs, seek immediate medical attention.

Heatstroke is a severe medical emergency that is indicated by a high body temperature (106+), and further identified by hot, dry skin, a rapid, strong pulse, possible loss of consciousness, and absence or lack of sweating. Immediately move a heatstroke victim to a cooler environment and try a cool bath, sponging, or the ice treatment described above to decrease the body temperature. **Do not give fluids**. Seek immediate medical attention. Delaying a trip to the hospital can be fatal.

Lightning: Although extreme temperatures can prove bothersome and even life-threatening on the trail, inclement weather, including lightning and thunderstorms, can be an equal menace. According to the National Lightning Safety Institute (NLSI), based in Louisville, Colorado, lightning causes more deaths in the United States than any other natural hazards.

Regardless of the month or region, no place is absolutely safe from lightning. The NLSI offers the following personal lightning safety tips. Lightning often precedes rain, so don't wait for the rain to begin before you stop running. Where possible, find shelter in a substantial building or in a car, truck, or a van with the windows completely shut. Avoid open spaces, water, and high ground. Avoid metal objects including electric wires, fences, machinery, motors, power tools, etc. Seeking shelter from lightning beneath canopies, small picnic or rain shelters, and trees is also unsafe. If lightning is striking nearby, crouch down with your feet together and your hands placed over your ears to minimize any hearing damage from thunder. The threat of lightning often activates the senses; your body hair will feel as if it is standing on end. In this case, immediately drop to the ground and lie flat. Avoid being closer than 15 feet to other people, and avoid running for 30 minutes after the last perceived lightning strike or thunderclap. When thunderstorms are in the area but not directly overhead, even when it is sunny or when clear sky is visible, the lightning threat can exist.

BIG DRY CREEK OPEN SPACE

WHAT THIS OPEN SPACE LACKS IN TERMS OF WIDTH, it makes up for in length. Running along Big Dry Creek, this conglomeration of open space and parkland covers over 800 acres and is over 12 miles long. Home to numerous owls, red-tailed hawks, and other birds, as well as coyotes, foxes, and wetland wildlife, this open space is a welcome retreat from the surrounding cities and suburbs.

BIG DRY CREEK TRAIL

This is an excellent yet little-known trail that runs for 12 miles along Big Dry Creek from Standley Lake Regional Park northeast all the way to I-25. Traveling through marshlands, wetlands, and open grasslands, this trail is excellent for faster or longer runs on a nice, wide gravel path.

THE RUN DOWN

START: Westminster City Park

OVERALL DISTANCE: 9.0 miles out and back

APPROXIMATE RUNNING TIME: 1 to 2 hours

DIFFICULTY: Green

ELEVATION GAIN: 269 feet

BEST SEASON TO RUN: Year-round, although summer can be hot and winter can be snowy

DOG FRIENDLY: Dogs must be on leash at all times

PARKING: Free

OTHER USERS: Hikers, mountain bikers

CELL PHONE COVERAGE: Good

MORE INFORMATION: www .ci.westminster.co.us/ ParksRec/TrailSystem/ BigDryCreekTrail.aspx

BIG DRY CREEK TRAIL

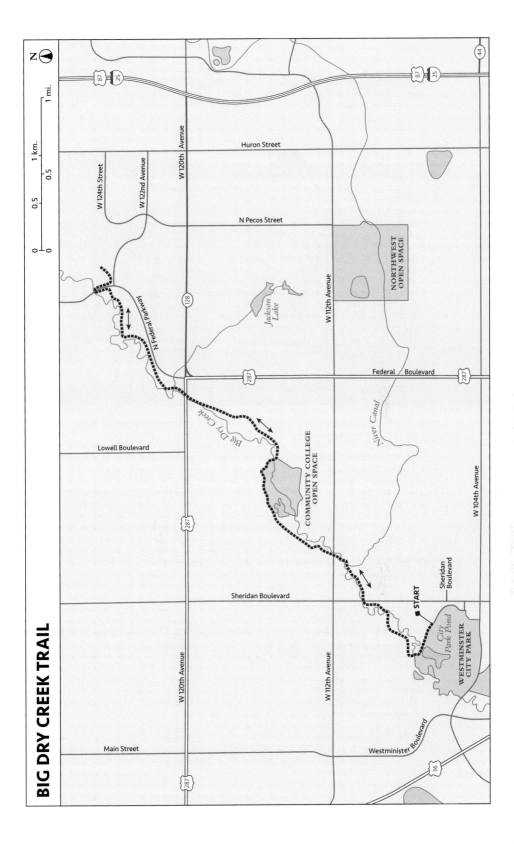

Open trails and open views are found on the Big Dry Creek Trail.
PHOTO BY PETER N. JONES

FINDING THE TRAILHEAD

Located directly off Sheridan Boulevard, the trailhead is situated on the far northwestern side of Westminster City Park. From US 36, exit onto 104th Avenue and turn right, following 104th as it curves around the south side of Westminster City Park. At West 104th Avenue and Sheridan Boulevard, turn left onto Sheridan, and then turn left again onto 105th Avenue into the park. Follow the signs around to the right of the recreation center and to the far parking lots; the trail starts from the western end of the parking lots.

RUN DESCRIPTION

This is a great run that many people don't think of. On a recent midweek morning, the author ran across only four other people on the trail, but was lucky enough to spot rabbits, a coyote, two red-tailed hawks, numerous waterfowl, and even a few mule deer tucked into the bushes. The trail runs for 12.0 miles, but only 9.0 are covered here—feel free to continue to get in a nice long run.

From the parking area, head down the gentle slope toward the creek, getting on the Big Dry Creek Trail at the sign. Cross the bridge and start running in a general northeastern direction as the trail rolls and winds along the edges of Big Dry Creek, which is on your right. A neighborhood subdivision is on your left. After the first mile the trail turns from cement to crushed gravel and dirt, and the open space widens, with large cotton-woods along the creek and various small ponds and marshlands in the surrounding areas. Continue on the trail for another 3.5 miles, passing under roadways and winding through mixed wetland terrain. Be sure to keep an eye out for hawks and owls perched in the cottonwoods, as well as other animals and waterfowl tucked in the ponds and marshes. At the 4.5-mile mark, turn around and follow the trail back to Westminster City Park. There are also many side trails that wind through and around the ponds and marshlands that you can take if you want to mix up the run a bit.

WINTER WEATHER HAZARDS

WEATHER HAZARDS VARY, depending on the season and the region.

Hypothermia: If you are exposed to severe cold without enough protection, then you are a prime candidate for hypothermia, a condition that occurs when body temperature drops below 95°F. The onset of symptoms is usually slow, with a gradual loss of mental acuity and physical ability. Additional symptoms include drowsiness, loss of coordination, uncontrollable shivering, and pale and cold skin. The person experiencing hypothermia, in fact, may be unaware that he or she is in a state that requires emergency medical treatment.

Frostbite: Another unpleasant condition that arises from extreme cold is frostbite, which causes tissue damage, primarily to extremities and exposed flesh. The three stages of frostbite include frostnip, superficial frostbite, and deep frostbite. Frostnip looks pale, feels cold, and is similar in physiology to a first-degree burn. Passive skin-to-skin contact is the best in-the-field warming method for frostnip. Superficial frostbite causes the skin to feel numb, waxy, and frozen, as ice crystals form in the skin cells while the rest of the skin remains flexible. Superficial frostbite may result in blisters within twenty-four hours after rewarming. Treatment for second-degree or superficial frostbite is rapid rewarming by immersion in warm (104° to 108°F) water. Unlike frostnip, the injury should not be rewarmed by simple application of heat. Proper rewarming is crucial to healing. Since frostnip and superficial frostbite can look almost identical prior to rewarming, it is not recommended that any heat be applied to any suspected frostbite other than skin-to-skin or the warm water treatment described above.

Deep frostbite is the most serious stage of frostbite. In this stage, blood vessels, muscles, tendons, nerves, and bone may be frozen. This stage will lead to permanent damage, blood clots, and sometimes gangrene in severe cases. No feeling is experienced in the affected area, the skin feels hard, and there is usually no blistering after rewarming. Loss of tissue to some extent is guaranteed in deep frostbite. However, even with deep frostbite, some frozen limbs may be saved if medical attention is obtained as soon as possible.

In all stages avoid massaging the affected area, and avoid application of high radiant heat sources such as the heat from stoves and fires. Wet clothes, high winds and the resulting wind chill, poor circulation, fatigue, and poor fluid and food intake exacerbate frostbite. In cold temperatures wear suitable clothing with appropriate layering, and protect more exposed areas such as your hands, feet, ears, and head.

APEX PARK

THE APEX PARK OPEN SPACE, located just off I-70 at the junction of Golden and Lakewood, may seem like one of the smaller open space parks in the Denver metro area, but it contains a great network of trails that are smartly designed, allowing you to run for several miles without repeating any trails. Long and narrow, the trails offer a diversity of terrain, from rocky climbs to smooth and flowy forested sections.

APEX OUT-AND-BACK

The aptly named Apex Trail follows the small creek flowing through Apex Park as it gradually ascends toward the west. Following the old Apex and Gregory Wagon Road, built in 1861 to serve miners, the trail is a great introduction to the park and provides runners with a smattering of the different types of terrain found in the park.

THE RUN DOWN

START: Apex Trailhead

OVERALL DISTANCE: 5.7 miles out and back

APPROXIMATE RUNNING TIME: 45 minutes to 1.5 hours

DIFFICULTY: Green

ELEVATION GAIN: 1,207 feet

BEST SEASON TO RUN: Spring and fall; summer is often hot and snow may be found in winter

DOG FRIENDLY: Dogs must be on leash at all times

PARKING: Free

CELL PHONE COVERAGE: Average

OTHER USERS: Hikers and mountain bikers

MORE INFORMATION: http://jeffco.us/open-space/parks/apex-park/

APEX OUT-AND-BACK

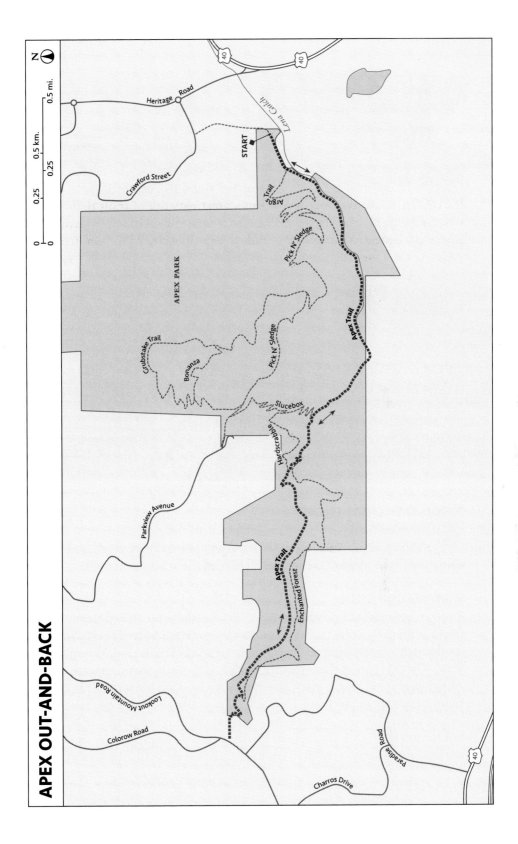

Running the trails at Apex Park is always a pleasure in the fall when the aspens are changing color.
PHOTO BY PETER N. JONES

FINDING THE TRAILHEAD

All trails for Apex Park start at the far northwestern corner of the public parking lot at Heritage Road and West Colfax Avenue. The site is also the location of the former Heritage Square Amusement Park.

RUN DESCRIPTION

The run up and back down the Apex Trail is the most straightforward found at the park. From the trailhead, it follows a seasonal creek as it winds up through the foothills, and reaches its terminus at Lookout Mountain Road. The first part of the run is a bit rocky, with a few technical sections. At just over the half-mile mark, the Pick N' Sledge Trail branches off to the right. Continue up the Apex Trail as it follows the creek through shaded sections. After 1.5 miles the steep switchbacks of Sluicebox Trail climb the hill to the right as the Apex Trail briefly passes through an open section with tall willows. Shortly after, the Enchanted Forest Trail branches off to the left, and the Hardscrabble Trail branches off to the right. Continue on the Apex Trail as it climbs away from the creek and passes through a beautiful, open meadow before coming back alongside the creek and entering another section of intermittent shade mixed with open meadows. The trail continues along the creek for another mile, passing through small aspen groves and open meadows before making a final climb up to its terminus between two houses. Turn around and enjoy the view looking back down the valley toward Denver before descending the same way that you came.

GRUBSTAKE TO HARDSCRABBLE LOOP

This run is a good alternative to the Apex Out-and-Back as it has about the same distance and elevation gain, but provides some excellent vistas to the north and south. The run climbs up the front of the mountain before looping around and descending the backside to make a nice loop.

THE RUN DOWN

START: Apex Trailhead

OVERALL DISTANCE: 5.5-mile loop

APPROXIMATE RUNNING TIME: 45 minutes to 1.5 hours

DIFFICULTY: Blue

ELEVATION GAIN: 1,132 feet

BEST SEASON TO RUN: Spring and fall; summer is often hot and snow may be found in winter

DOG FRIENDLY: Dogs must be on leash at all times

PARKING: Free

OTHER USERS: Hikers and mountain bikers

CELL PHONE COVERAGE: Average

MORE INFORMATION: http:// jeffco.us/open-space/parks/ apex-park/

FINDING THE TRAILHEAD

All trails for Apex Park start at the far northwestern corner of the public parking lot at Heritage Road and West Colfax Avenue. The site is also the location of the former Heritage Square Amusement Park.

RUN DESCRIPTION

The network of trails looping up and around the small mountain in the front of Apex Park provides excellent vistas, shady sections through pine forests, open meadows, and some fun and fast descents.

Start the run on the main trail leaving the parking area, but then quickly turn off to the left, onto the Argos Trail as it switchbacks up the east face of the mountain through open prairie and shrubs. Just before reaching the

GRUBSTAKE TO HARDSCRABBLE LOOP

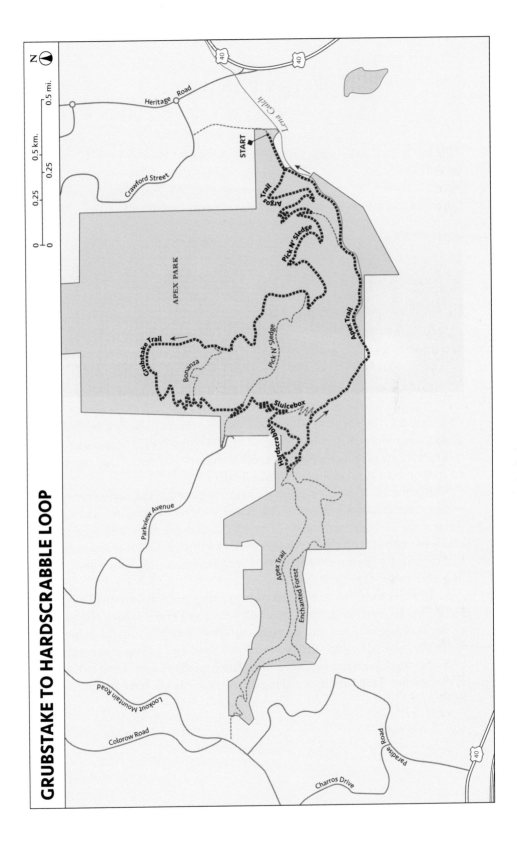

START

Lena Gulch

Heritage Road

Crawford Street

APEX PARK

Argos Trail

Pick N' Sledge

Grubstake Trail

Bonanza

Pick N' Sledge

Apex Trail

Sluicebox

Hardscrabble

Parkview Avenue

Apex Trail

Enchanted Forest

Lookout Mountain Road

Colorow Road

Paradise Road

Charros Drive

N

0   0.25   0.5 km.
0   0.25   0.5 mi.

Running the trails on a misty, cloud-filled morning.
PHOTO BY PETER N. JONES

1.0-mile mark, the Argos Trail ends and dumps you onto the Pick N' Sledge Trail; turn right and continue to climb up the rocky trail. There are a few technical portions filled with small rocky sections before the trail reaches an apex and encounters the Grubstake Trail.

The Grubstake Trail is a blast, as it contours around to the north through rolling open meadows, providing spectacular views to the north and east. Around the 2.5-mile mark the trail enters a nice, dense forest and begins to climb switchbacks up the north side of the mountain. Grunt through this section, passing the turnoff to the Bonanza Trail on the left, before heading downhill toward the west.

At 3.2 miles the Grubstake Trail ends, spitting you out onto the Pick N' Sledge Trail. Turn right, run a hundred yards, and make a sharp left turn as the trail begins a fun and fast descent down into the canyon. After a half-mile turn right onto the Hardscrabble Trail and follow it around as it drops you down onto the Apex Trail (mentioned above). Turn left and take the Apex Trail back down along the creek to the trailhead to complete the loop.

APEX OUTER LOOP

The Apex Outer Loop is exactly what it sounds like: a hard run that covers the entire park in one large loop. This trail showcases the best the park has to offer—rocky climbs, smooth and flowy singletrack, shaded forest, and open meadows.

THE RUN DOWN

START: Apex Trailhead

OVERALL DISTANCE: 8.0-mile loop

APPROXIMATE RUNNING TIME: 1 to 2 hours

DIFFICULTY: Black

ELEVATION GAIN: 1,654 feet

BEST SEASON TO RUN: Spring and fall; summer is often hot and snow may be found in winter

DOG FRIENDLY: Dogs must be on leash at all times

PARKING: Free

OTHER USERS: Hikers and mountain bikers

CELL PHONE COVERAGE: Average

MORE INFORMATION: http://jeffco.us/open-space/parks/apex-park/

FINDING THE TRAILHEAD

All trails for Apex Park start at the far northwestern corner of the public parking lot at Heritage Road and West Colfax Avenue. The site is also the location of the former Heritage Square Amusement Park.

RUN DESCRIPTION

This run combines the two runs previously described, but throws in the Enchanted Forest Trail to finish off the loop. To start, follow the description for the Grubstake to Hardscrabble Loop. When you get to the Hardscrabble/Apex Trail junction, instead of turning left and running down the canyon, turn right and gently climb up the canyon. Initially the trail passes through a nice open meadow before joining back up with the creek, passing through interspersed aspen groves, meadows, and creek-side growth. At the 5.0-mile mark, the Apex Trail reaches the junction with

APEX OUTER LOOP

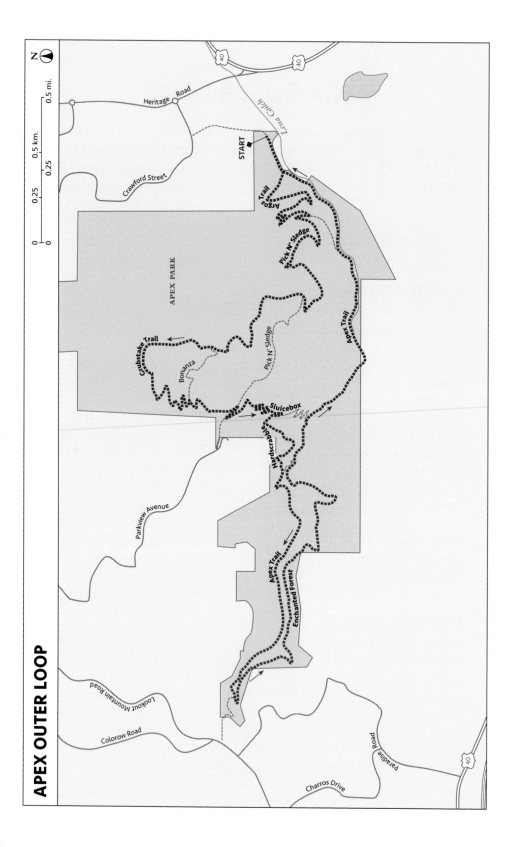

The trails found at Apex Park offer a variety of terrain and vistas, even in the winter.
PHOTO BY PETER N. JONES

the Enchanted Forest Trail. Turn onto the Enchanted Forest Trail and follow it back to the south and then east, as it meanders through dense, shady forests. This part of the run is always a treat, as the trail is fairly smooth and rolling, making for a fun and fast section.

After a quick 1.5 miles, the Enchanted Forest Trail ends and dumps you back out onto the Apex Trail next to the creek. Continue down the Apex Trail as it descends alongside the creek, following it back to the trailhead to complete the loop.

ALTITUDE

SINCE MANY OF THE TRAILS IN THIS GUIDE ARE AT HIGHER elevations (6,000 feet and greater), it is important to understand the physiological effects that come with the breathtaking—literally and figuratively—beauty at or above 5,280 feet (a mile high). Running at higher elevations is physically demanding and it is worthwhile to acknowledge the risks and challenges accompanying high altitude running, especially if you have come from sea level and are running at a high elevation without first acclimatizing.

EFFECTS OF ALTITUDE ON THE BODY'S PERFORMANCE

Exertion at higher altitudes is more difficult than at sea level because of the reduced partial pressure of oxygen as elevation rises. The decrease in oxygen pressure impairs the oxygenation of blood flowing through the lungs, which ultimately results in a corresponding diminished oxygen supply to working muscles. Studies by the Federation of Sport at Altitude (now the International Skyrunning Federation) have shown that the lack of oxygen at elevations above 10,000 feet translates to 25-40% less muscle power (depending on the subject).

The human body requires a constant supply of oxygen from ambient air to maintain the process of aerobic metabolism. Even though the percentage of oxygen in the air remains constant regardless of altitude, the decrease in pressure relative to an increase in altitude translates into a diminished oxygen-hemoglobin association. In short, the higher the altitude, the less oxygen carried in the bloodstream, making it harder for your muscles and lungs to do their jobs.

PHYSIOLOGICAL ADAPTATION TO ALTITUDE

To compensate for the reduced oxygen delivery at altitude, the heart must work harder and faster to maintain the same absolute performance or pace. The heart compensates for the diminution of oxygen through an increase in cardiac output, or the amount of blood pumped by each heartbeat.

Blood composition is another way the body compensates for altitude. After fourteen to sixty days of altitude acclimatization, the body produces more red blood cells and hemoglobin—the iron-protein compound that transports oxygen.

Altitude also causes the kidneys to increase production of erythropoietin, or EPO, which stimulates bone marrow production to increase both the concentration of red cells in the blood and total plasma volume. EPO is a favorite substance for drug-doping endurance competitors trying to find a shortcut to greater fitness.

An additional adaptation to altitude is that working muscle tissue learns to rely on more fatty acids rather than the common glycogen source of energy fuel. These gradual adaptations result in a reduction of the cardiac output required for oxygen delivery during exercise.

The virtues of altitude training for endurance athletes have been touted since the 1968 Olympics in Mexico City, where it was established that performance at high altitude requires training at high altitude. Studies have shown, however, that the physiological response to altitude training varies widely, depending upon individual characteristics. Accordingly, the following discussion of training at altitude is general in nature.

We recommend that individuals customize any altitude training based upon advice from a qualified coach, exercise physiologist, or other certified trainer. And remember, very few paved roads exist above 12,000 feet—in fact, in Colorado there are only two, one to the summit of Mount Evans, the other to the summit of Pikes Peak—so running trails is almost mandatory if you want to do more extreme altitude training.

BERGEN PEAK AND ELK MEADOW

THE ELK MEADOW AND BERGEN PEAK OPEN SPACE PARKS, located just outside of Evergreen in the foothills above Denver, are true gems. At just over 7,500 feet in elevation, the park is often cooler than parks closer to Denver, yet it is only a fifteen-minute drive from the west edge of the city. With a large, open meadow and a 9,700-foot summit, the Elk Meadow/Bergen Peak open space provides ample opportunities for trail running over a wide variety of terrain.

ELK MEADOW/MEADOW VIEW LOOP

This fantastic loop circles the large, open meadow found at the base of Bergen Peak. In the summer the meadow is full of wildflowers, while in the fall it is not uncommon to see elk grazing in the tall grasses.

THE RUN DOWN

START: Lewis Ridge Trailhead

OVERALL DISTANCE: 5.1-mile loop

APPROXIMATE RUNNING TIME: 35 minutes to 1 hour

DIFFICULTY: Blue

ELEVATION GAIN: 638 feet

BEST SEASON TO RUN: Summer and fall; winter can be snowy, and spring can be muddy

DOG FRIENDLY: Dogs must be on leash at all times

PARKING: Free

OTHER USERS: Hikers, mountain bikers

CELL PHONE COVERAGE: Average

MORE INFORMATION: http://jeffco.us/open-space/parks/elk-meadow-park/

ELK MEADOW/MEADOW VIEW LOOP

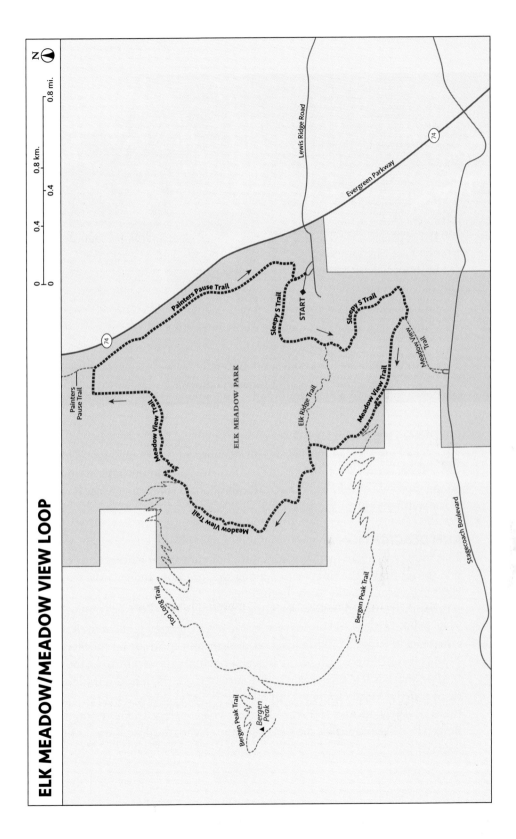

Climbing hills is a must on the trails around Denver; doing it with friends makes them less steep.
PHOTO BY PETER N. JONES

FINDING THE TRAILHEAD

The Lewis Ridge Trailhead is located just off CO 74 on Lewis Ridge Road. From I-70, take exit 252 and follow CO 74 to the large meadow on the west side of the road. The trailhead is located on Lewis Ridge Road, at the southern end of the meadow.

RUN DESCRIPTION

This loop can be run in either direction, but running it clockwise allows you to run down the final section along the meadow, and gets the major climbing out of the way at the beginning.

From the trailhead, follow the Sleepy S Trail as it heads toward Bergen Peak, before it turns and begins to wind through the open pine forest. At 0.5 mile, the Elk Ridge Trail branches off to the right; continue on the Sleep S Trail as it continues south before it begins to climb up west into the forest.

After another 0.6 mile, a side trail comes in from the left; the trail now turns into the Meadow View Trail as it continues west into the forest. Here the trail levels off and rolls through the woods before encountering the Bergen Peak Trail split on the left. Continue on the Meadow View Trail as it continues to roll through the forest and intermixed open meadows, passing the Elk Ridge Trail junction on the right at mile 2.0.

Eventually the trail reaches the northern edge of the meadow and begins to curve to the east, passing the Too Long Trail junction on the left and then the Founders Trail junction on the right. Continue on the Meadow View Trail over a small rise before turning to the east and joining the Painters Pause Trail. Turn right onto the Painters Pause Trail and run downhill along this trail through the open meadow back south to the trailhead to finish the loop.

BERGEN PEAK/TOO LONG/ MEADOW VIEW LOOP

This fun but hard loop covers most of the park and travels through a variety of terrain and ecosystems. Although it doesn't reach the summit of Bergen Peak, this loop still packs a punch and is a good test of your fitness.

THE RUN DOWN

START: Lewis Ridge Trailhead

OVERALL DISTANCE: 8.6-mile loop

APPROXIMATE RUNNING TIME: 1 to 2 hours

DIFFICULTY: Black

ELEVATION GAIN: 1,786 feet

BEST SEASON TO RUN: Summer and fall; winter can be snowy, and spring can be muddy

DOG FRIENDLY: Dogs must be on leash at all times

PARKING: Free

OTHER USERS: Hikers, mountain bikers

CELL PHONE COVERAGE: Average

MORE INFORMATION: http://jeffco.us/open-space/parks/elk-meadow-park/

FINDING THE TRAILHEAD

The Lewis Ridge Trailhead is located just off CO 74 on Lewis Ridge Road. From I-70, take exit 252 and follow CO 74 to the large meadow on the west side of the road. The trailhead is located on Lewis Ridge Road, at the southern end of the meadow.

RUN DESCRIPTION

This hard run takes you up near the summit of Bergen Peak, and it also provides a solid test of your fitness as it has some climbing and some downhill, as well as some rolling terrain.

From the trailhead follow the Sleepy S Trail west as it heads through the meadow before turning to the south. At 0.5 mile, the Elk Ridge Trail joins the Sleepy S Trail—take note, as you will be coming down the Elk Ridge Trail at the end of the loop. Continue on the Sleep S Trail as it winds along,

BERGEN PEAK/TOO LONG/MEADOW VIEW LOOP

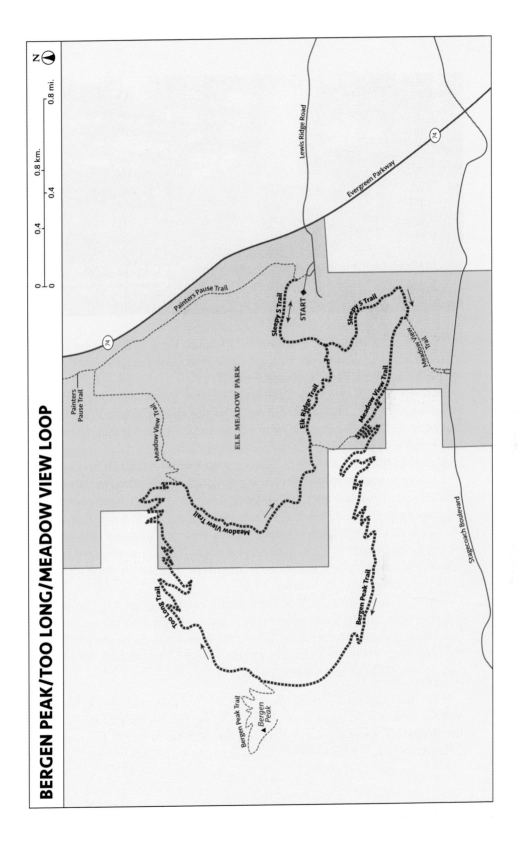

N

0   0.4   0.8 km.
0   0.4   0.8 mi.

Lewis Ridge Road

74

Evergreen Parkway

Painters Pause Trail

Sleepy S Trail

START

Sleepy S Trail

74

Painters Pause Trail

Meadow View Trail

Meadow View Trail

ELK MEADOW PARK

Elk Ridge Trail

Meadow View Trail

Meadow View Trail

Meadow View Trail

Too Long Trail

Bergen Peak Trail

Bergen Peak Trail

Bergen Peak

Bergen Peak Trail

Stagecoach Boulevard

Runners bomb down a hill
on a cool, fall morning.
PHOTO BY PETER N. JONES

and then climbs, before turning into the Meadow View Trail. Follow the Meadow View Trail as it rolls through thick pine forest before encountering the Bergen Peak Trail on your left at mile 1.8.

Turn onto the Bergen Peak Trail and begin the long climb toward the top of Bergen Peak. This climb can easily be run as it switchbacks up the mountain for 2.7 miles. Finally, near the top, the trail levels out and passes by a small rocky ridge. Not far beyond, on the left, is the short out-and-back trail to the true summit of Bergen Peak. You can take this out-and-back path if you want to tag the summit; it will add 2 miles total to the run.

Otherwise, continue on the Too Long Trail as it heads north before beginning the fun and sometimes technical descent back down toward the meadow, almost 2,000 feet below. As you reach the meadow, you will encounter the Meadow View Trail on your right. Turn onto this trail and follow it south as it skirts the western edge of the meadow through intermixed forest and meadow habitat.

Finally, after 7.5 miles, you will encounter the Elk Ridge Trail on the left; turn onto this trail and follow it as it descends back into the meadow and connects you with the Sleepy S Trail at the spot you encountered near the beginning of the run. Turn left onto the Sleepy S Trail and run 0.5 mile back to the trailhead to complete the loop.

BEAR CREEK LAKE PARK

BEAR CREEK LAKE PARK, LOCATED ON THE WESTERN EDGE OF DENVER, is a gem for trail runners. Consisting of a number of trails that wind through open meadows, cottonwoods, and mixed terrain, Bear Creek Lake Park is one of the few trail networks in Denver that does not require a lot of climbing. Perfect for easy runs, longer runs, or speed workouts, the trails in Bear Creek Lake Park are home to abundant wildlife including owls, hawks, deer, and water birds.

MOUNT CARBON LOOP

This is the main loop in the park, following a series of trails through dense cottonwoods and open cottonwoods, with a short climb to the top of Mount Carbon, the highest point in the park. With excellent views in all directions, this loop is a great tour of the trail network in the park.

THE RUN DOWN

START: Skunk Hollow Trailhead

OVERALL DISTANCE: 6.6-mile loop

APPROXIMATE RUNNING TIME: 1 to 1.5 hours

DIFFICULTY: Green

ELEVATION GAIN: 616 feet

BEST SEASON TO RUN: Year-round, although summer can be hot and winter can be snowy

DOG FRIENDLY: Dogs must be on leash at all times

PARKING: An entrance fee is charged

OTHER USERS: Hikers, mountain bikers, equestrians

CELL PHONE COVERAGE: Good

MORE INFORMATION: www .lakewood.org/bclp/

MOUNT CARBON LOOP

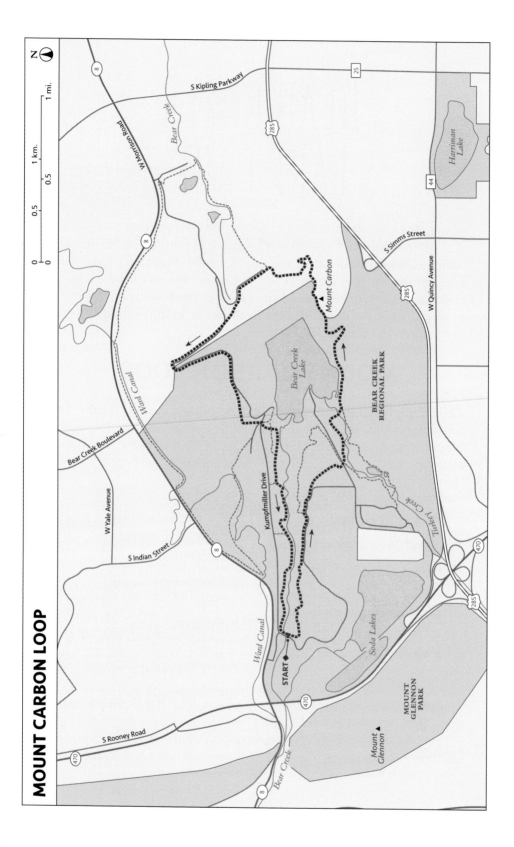

Tara Jones runs through Bear Creek Lake Park on a cool, fall morning.
PHOTO BY PETER N. JONES

FINDING THE TRAILHEAD

The Skunk Hollow parking area and trailhead are located just inside the park entrance. From C-470 on the west side of Denver, take the Morrison Road exit and turn east, back toward Denver. The park entrance is about 0.5 mile from the C-470 exit on Morrison Road; turn right and pass through the entrance station. Immediately turn right and cross Bear Creek; the Skunk Hollow parking lot and trailhead is on the right.

RUN DESCRIPTION

From the parking area, cross over the road and get onto the marked Mount Carbon Loop trail. This trail will lead you around the park; it is marked the entire way but crosses several other trails so it is important to pay attention at junctions.

After 0.5 mile the Mount Carbon Loop encounters and parallels one of the inner park roads; continue on the singletrack trail for another 0.5 mile before the trail leaves the road and crosses some open grasslands. At mile 1.2 the trail crosses another inner park road and then heads down a small hill into the cottonwoods. Run along a sandy section of trail before crossing a small bridge at mile 1.6, and then continue through a large open prairie on the south side of Bear Creek Lake.

At the 2.0-mile mark the trail begins the short but steep climb up Mount Carbon via two switchbacks. From the summit of Mount Carbon take in

FLORA AND FAUNA

Trail runners often venture into areas teeming with wildlife. The potential for animal sightings varies with the season, region, and terrain, as well as the amount of human traffic on a particular route. Even if a run is void of an animal encounter, scat, broken tree limbs, or a carcass can provide remnant evidence of an animal presence along a trail. Be aware of the wildlife populations in any area in which you plan to run. Take the time to gather information and educate yourself on the best way to react during an encounter.

the views in all directions before continuing east on the trail as it passes near a golf course, then begins a fun, rolling descent down the other side of the dam.

At the bottom of the descent the trail turns into a paved path with dirt on the side; continue running on the trail, now heading north as it climbs up the gentle slope toward the north side of the dam. At mile 4.1 the trail reaches the top of the climb and passes through a gate before turning south and heading back down toward the lake on dirt singletrack that parallels the road.

At mile 4.6 the trail leaves the side of the road and passes through more open grasslands toward a small gulch, at which point it heads down toward the lake. Follow the trail down, cross over the road toward the parking area, and continue on the trail as it enters a dense stand of cottonwoods (mile 5). Turn west and follow the trail as it winds through the cottonwoods, with Bear Creek on your left, for another 1.5 mile before the trail takes you back over the creek and to the Skunk Hollow parking area to complete the loop.

BEAR CREEK LAKE FULL LOOP

This loop covers the entire Bear Creek Lake Park, offering a longer trail run without too much vertical gain. Perfect for long runs, this loop has three small creek crossings that give the feeling of a more mountainous trail run; coupled with the abundant wildlife found in the park, this loop is perfect for a weekend day on the trails.

THE RUN DOWN

START: Skunk Hollow Trailhead

OVERALL DISTANCE: 12.5-mile loop

APPROXIMATE RUNNING TIME: 2 to 3 hours

DIFFICULTY: Blue

ELEVATION GAIN: 892 feet

BEST SEASON TO RUN: Year-round, although summer can be hot and winter can be snowy

DOG FRIENDLY: Dogs must be on leash at all times

PARKING: An entrance fee is charged

OTHER USERS: Hikers, mountain bikers, equestrians

CELL PHONE COVERAGE: Good

MORE INFORMATION: www .lakewood.org/bclp/

FINDING THE TRAILHEAD

The Skunk Hollow parking area and trailhead are located just inside the park entrance. From C-470 on the west side of Denver, take the Morrison Road exit and turn east, back toward Denver. The park entrance is about 0.5 mile from the C-470 exit on Morrison Road; turn right and pass through the entrance station. Immediately turn right and cross Bear Creek; the Skunk Hollow parking lot and trailhead is on the right.

RUN DESCRIPTION

This loop covers most of the trails found within the park, plus a small section outside the park, making for a nice long loop. From the Skunk Hollow parking area, cross the road and start running on the Mount Carbon Loop trail. Follow this trail east through cottonwoods and open grasslands. After

BEAR CREEK LAKE FULL LOOP

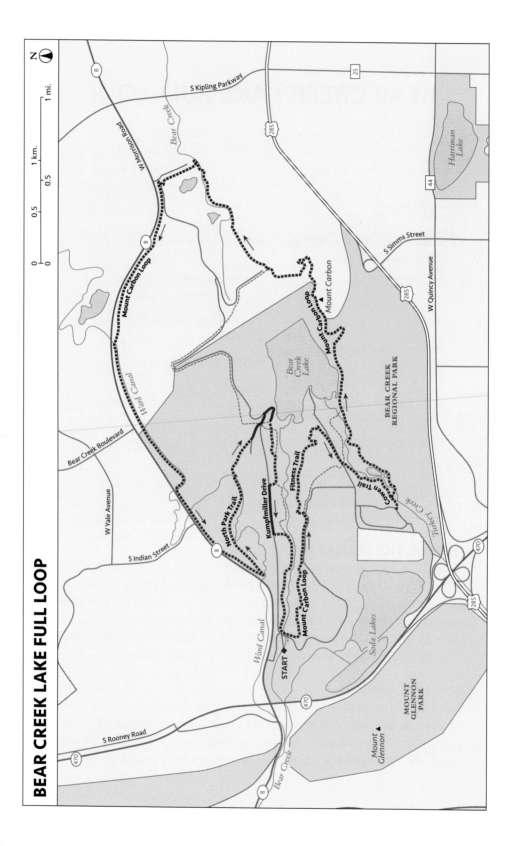

A runner getting in a tempo workout on one of the many trails found in Bear Creek Lake Park.
PHOTO BY PETER N. JONES

0.5 mile the trail reaches an inner park road and parallels it for another 0.5 mile. Follow the roadway to a small junction at 0.8 mile, then turn left down a small hill and reach the Fitness Trail.

Turn right and run on the Fitness Trail, which is a wide gravel path that rolls through a large open meadow before heading up a small rise and encountering another inner park road. The Fitness Trail turns west and parallels the road briefly before crossing it and turning down a small hill (mile 1.8).

Here, the run turns onto the Cowen Trail as it passes through cottonwoods along a small creek in a southwesterly direction. Continue on the Cowen Trail as it winds through the cottonwoods before crossing the creek and turning back east (mile 2.3). Stay on the Cowen Trail as it heads back east on the other side of the small creek, passing a small pond and then reaching the Mount Carbon Loop trail (mile 2.7).

Turn onto the Mount Carbon Loop and follow it across the large open grassland before climbing up to the top of Mount Carbon. Take in the views in all directions before continuing east on the Mount Carbon trail, running down the backside of the dam and turning onto the Stone House Trail (mile 4.7). The Stone House Trail winds through more cottonwoods on the southern side of the golf course, crossing Bear Creek three times (don't be shy about getting your feet wet—this is what trail running is all about) before ending at the bike path.

Turn left onto the bike path and follow it briefly as it heads north and crosses a road before turning left back onto the singletrack trail that parallels Morrison Road. This long section of trail rolls through a large grassland area with great views of the foothills to the west and south; at mile 6.0 the trail drops below the road and parallels an irrigation ditch.

At mile 8.0 the trail connects up with the North Park Trail; turn onto the North Park Trail and follow it as it runs west again, paralleling Morrison Road. The trail climbs over a small rise before heading back down, and then turning sharply from west to east. Follow the North Park Trail as it rolls through more open grasslands before turning south and ending at the large parking area on the northern shore of Bear Creek Lake. Turn onto the Mount Carbon Loop and follow it west as it winds through cottonwoods for another 1.5 mile to return to the Skunk Hollow parking area and the start of the loop.

DEER CREEK CANYON AND SOUTH VALLEY PARKS

COMBINED, THESE TWO OPEN SPACE PARKS hold some of the best trail running in the Denver area. Deer Creek offers challenging climbs and vistas, while South Valley is home to rolling grasslands and spectacular red rock formations. Often quiet, these trails really shine in the fall when the Gambel oaks, cottonwoods, and grasslands blaze with color, and make for outstanding runs just minutes from central Denver.

PLYMOUTH MOUNTAIN LOOP

This is a challenging yet worthwhile loop run to the top of Plymouth Mountain, where you are rewarded with outstanding views to the north, east, and south. Encompassing a challenging ascent and a fast and fun descent through Gambel oak, ponderosa pine forests, and open meadows, this run has it all.

THE RUN DOWN

START: Grizzly Drive Trailhead

OVERALL DISTANCE: 6.7-mile loop

APPROXIMATE RUNNING TIME: 1 to 1.75 hours

DIFFICULTY: Blue

ELEVATION GAIN: 1,600 feet

BEST SEASON TO RUN: Summer and fall; winter can be snowy and spring can be muddy

DOG FRIENDLY: Dogs must be on leash at all times

PARKING: Free

OTHER USERS: Hikers, mountain bikers

CELL PHONE COVERAGE: Average

MORE INFORMATION: http:// jeffco.us/open-space/parks/ deer-creek-canyon-park/

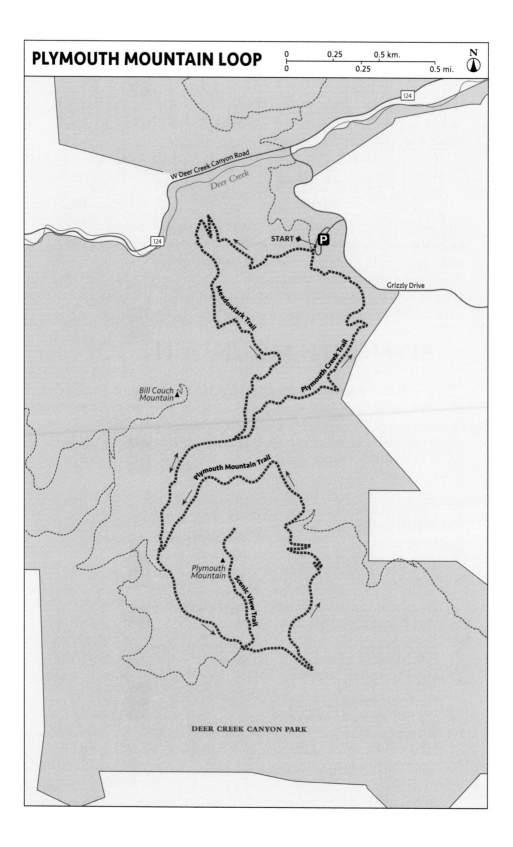

There are many excellent views and vantage points along the trails at Deer Creek.
PHOTO BY PETER N. JONES

FINDING THE TRAILHEAD

The Grizzly Drive Trailhead is located directly off Grizzly Drive. From C-470 take the Kipling exit and turn west (right) onto West Ute Avenue, and then west (right) onto Deer Creek Canyon Road. Follow Deer Creek Canyon Road into the canyon, and shortly after entering, turn left onto Grizzly Drive. Drive up the short but steep hill, and then turn right into the large parking lot; the trails start from the west side of the parking lot.

RUN DESCRIPTION

This run is basically a figure eight with a short out-and-back in the middle. It can be run clockwise or counterclockwise, but starting the figure eight clockwise on the Meadowlark Trail allows for a more gradual warm-up and is the route described here.

From the parking lot run west on the Meadowlark Trail as it gently ascends through the open grassland and Gambel oak. The trail switchbacks up the hillside, heading north before eventually turning south toward Plymouth Creek. At 1.5 miles the Meadowlark Trail ends; turn right and begin climbing the Plymouth Creek Trail as it climbs steeply up "The Wall"—a short but steep section with stairsteps.

After "The Wall" the trail mellows out but continues to climb, passing the Plymouth Mountain Trail junction on the left at mile 2. At mile 2.2 a junction is encountered, with the Plymouth Creek Trail going right and the Plymouth Mountain Trail continuing straight and uphill; leave the

Plymouth Creek Trail and follow the Plymouth Mountain Trail as it continues to climb past small, open meadows.

At the top of the climb (mile 2.5), the Homesteader Trail branches off to the right, while just a few feet past is the Scenic View Trail, an out-and-back trail to the summit of Plymouth Mountain. Turn left onto the Scenic View Trail and run it out to the rocky outcrop for spectacular views in all directions. After taking in the amazing views, run back to the Plymouth Mountain Trail and follow it left and down as it winds down the south and east sides of Plymouth Mountain through mixed Gambel oak and ponderosa pine forests.

At 5.1 miles the Plymouth Mountain Trail ends and dumps you back onto the Plymouth Creek Trail, which you already ascended. Turn right and bomb down the steep and semitechnical trail, passing the Meadowlark Trail that you also ascended earlier. Make sure to keep a little bit of energy in the tank, as the Plymouth Creek Trail is all downhill except for the last 0.5 mile back to the parking lot to complete the run.

SOUTH VALLEY LOOP

This fun and fast loop rolls through open meadows and alongside amazing red rock formations. Deer, coyotes, and birds of prey are common sights on this loop.

THE RUN DOWN

START: South Valley Trailhead

OVERALL DISTANCE: 3.9-mile loop

APPROXIMATE RUNNING TIME: 30 minutes to 1 hour

DIFFICULTY: Green

ELEVATION GAIN: 484 feet

BEST SEASON TO RUN: Spring, winter, and fall; summer can be hot

DOG FRIENDLY: Dogs must be on leash at all times

PARKING: Free

OTHER USERS: Hikers, mountain bikers, equestrians

CELL PHONE COVERAGE: Good

MORE INFORMATION: http://jeffco.us/open-space/parks/south-valley-park/

FINDING THE TRAILHEAD

The South Valley Trailhead is located directly off Valley Road. From C-470 take the Kipling exit and turn west (right) onto West Ute Avenue, then west (right) onto Deer Creek Canyon Road. Follow Deer Creek Canyon Road into the canyon, and shortly after entering turn right onto Valley Road. Follow Valley Road as it winds north through the valley to the trailhead, located on the north side of the valley.

RUN DESCRIPTION

The loop through South Valley is a fun, fast run passing spectacular red rock formations and open meadows. It can be run either clockwise or counterclockwise; the clockwise direction is described here.

From the main parking area, climb up the stairs and start running on the Coyote Song Trail, passing through the large sandstone rock formations. The trail then passes through an open meadow as it heads up toward the hogback. At 0.6 mile, the Coyote Song Trail encounters a spur, turn off

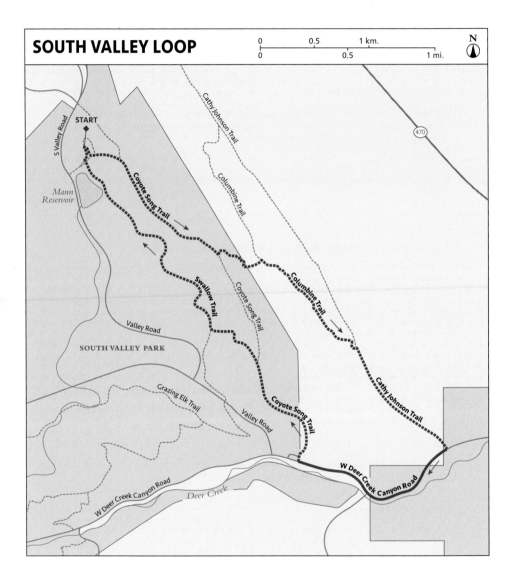

SOUTH VALLEY LOOP

0   0.5   1 km.
0   0.5   1 mi.

N

470

START
S Valley Road
Cathy Johnson Trail
Columbine Trail
Coyote Song Trail
Mann Reservoir
Swallow Trail
Coyote Song Trail
Columbine Trail
Valley Road
SOUTH VALLEY PARK
Grazing Elk Trail
Valley Road
Cathy Johnson Trail
Coyote Song Trail
W Deer Creek Canyon Road
W Deer Creek Canyon Road
Deer Creek

Numerous sandstone rock formations are found in South Valley Park.
PHOTO BY PETER N. JONES

onto this spur trail, cross over the hogback, and turn right onto the Columbine Trail.

You are now in a hidden valley between two hogbacks, lending a remote feeling to the run. Follow the Columbine Trail south as it descends through the valley, meeting up with the Cathy Johnson Trail at 1.5 miles. The Cathy Johnson Trail is a wide gravel path that continues down the valley to Deer Creek Canyon Road at mile 1.8, the low point on the run. Once you hit the road, turn right (west) and follow the small social trail that parallels the road to mile 2.4, where you will encounter the Coyote Song Trail and the southern trailhead for South Valley Park.

Turn right (north) onto the Coyote Song Trail and begin the gradual climb back toward the parking lot and northern trailhead, as the trail winds through open grasslands and past more red rock formations. At 2.8 miles, turn left onto the Swallow Trail and follow it north back to the trailhead, past the small reservoir, to complete the loop.

HIGHLANDS RANCH OPEN SPACE

SITTING AT THE SOUTHERN EDGE OF DENVER, Highlands Ranch offers some of the best open space trail running in the Denver area. With wide expanses, open prairie and grasslands, and interesting views from various small mesa tops, the trail network and open spaces south of Highlands Ranch have something for every type of runner.

HRCA BACKCOUNTRY WILDERNESS HALF-MARATHON

Every November the Highlands Ranch Community Association (HRCA) Backcountry Wilderness Half-Marathon is held on the open space just south of Highlands Ranch. Running official race courses is one of the best ways to judge your fitness without paying an entry fee, and the HRCA course is one of the best in the Denver area, with rolling terrain, hard climbs, and grand vistas.

THE RUN DOWN

START: Paintbrush Park

OVERALL DISTANCE: 13.1 miles

APPROXIMATE RUNNING TIME: 1.5 to 3 hours

DIFFICULTY: Blue

ELEVATION GAIN: 1,210 feet

BEST SEASON TO RUN: Year-round, although summer can be hot and winter can be snowy

DOG FRIENDLY: Dogs must be on leash at all times

PARKING: Free

OTHER USERS: Hikers, mountain bikers, equestrians

CELL PHONE COVERAGE: Good

MORE INFORMATION: http://highlandsranch.org/services/parks-open-space/trails/

HRCA BACKCOUNTRY WILDERNESS HALF-MARATHON

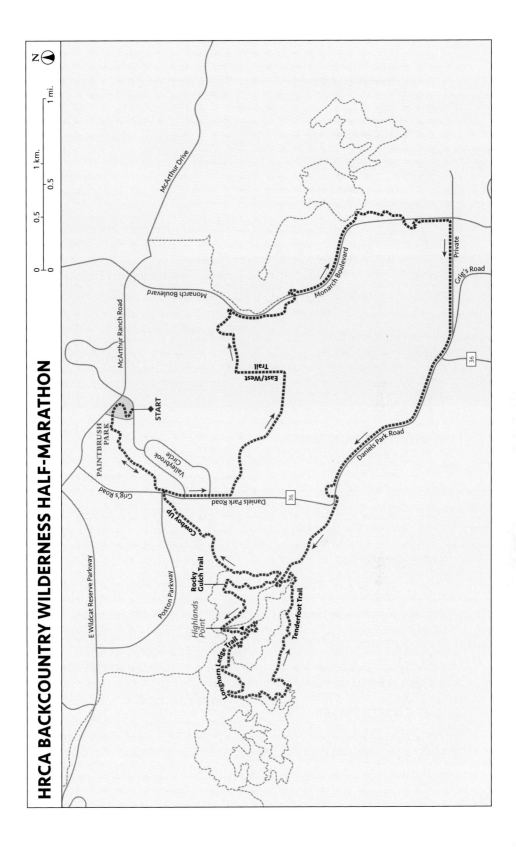

A group of runners enjoys a
beautiful summer day on the trails.
PHOTO BY TODD STRAKA

FINDING THE TRAILHEAD

From C-470 take the University Boulevard exit and turn south. Follow University Boulevard to Wildcat Reserve Boulevard and turn right. Stay on Wildcat Reserve Boulevard to McArthur Ranch Road. Turn left on McArthur Ranch Road and follow it to Paintbrush Park, located on the right just past the recreation center.

RUN DESCRIPTION

This is a great run to test out your fitness, especially if you are training for a longer trail race or just want to see how you would do in a half-marathon.

From the parking area, start by following the paved bike path, called the West Big Dry Creek Path, through the neighborhood as it winds out to the open space. At 0.8 mile, turn onto Grigs Road and follow it a short way before turning left (east) onto a crush gravel path. Follow the gravel path as it rolls through the open country, making a hard left at 2.0 miles and a hard left at 2.3 miles, before rolling down and connecting up with the Douglas County East/West Trail.

Turn right onto the East/West Trail as it parallels Monarch Road briefly before crossing the road at mile 3.3. Continue on the trail as it rolls and winds through mixed grassland and Gambel oak terrain before crossing back over the road at mile 4.5.

At 4.8 miles, the trail turns west and runs along the backside of a small neighborhood before encountering and paralleling Grigs Road. Continue on the singletrack along Grigs Road before crossing over and getting onto the East/West Regional Trail at mile 7.0.

After a nice mellow descent, turn left off the East/West Regional Trail and onto the Highlands Point trail system (7.6 miles). Continue on the trail system as it continues to descend through Gambel oak and mixed scrub.

At 9.0 miles you are at the lowest point, and the trail begins to climb to the highest point in the Highlands Ranch open space, which you reach at mile 10.5. Enjoy the spectacular views in all directions before beginning the final 3.0-mile descent back to the West Big Dry Creek Trail (11.5 miles). Turn onto West Big Dry Creek Trail and follow it back through the neighborhoods to Paintbrush Park.

Recovery, Rest, and Common Sense

MORE IS NOT ALWAYS BETTER. This is sometimes the most difficult lesson for trail runners to fully absorb. Failure to learn the lesson leads to acute injury or chronic suboptimal performance. Even ultrarunners know that some rest, even if only active rest through cross-training, enhances their running performance. Just as the need exists to integrate recovery and rest into repeat or interval training to get the most from each repeat or interval, periods of recovery and rest should be integrated into an overall training schedule. It often takes more discipline to take a day off than to go hard or long.

With proper recovery and rest, trail runners are able to attack hard days and make them worthwhile. Without recovery and rest, the pace of hard runs and easy runs will be approximately the same, and very little benefit will result from either. If you are the type who is likely to overdo it, keep a running log or journal to track your daily runs, noting time, effort, mileage, and other pertinent factors such as weather, cross-training activities, sleep, diet, work load, emotional state, stress level, terrain and, if you know them, altitude and heart rate. Those daily entries will force you to face the question of whether you are doing quality runs, as opposed to sheer quantity. The diary will also give an indication of whether you are overtraining. When you notice progress in your running, you will be in a better position to recall and evaluate what factors worked to produce that success.

Another alternative for those who lack the discipline for proper recovery and rest is to get a coach. Although not many coaches specialize in trail training, a good running coach will be able to help develop a customized training schedule that takes into consideration a runner's personal strengths and weaknesses. A coach should also help integrate recovery days and rest into your training.

Only so much fuel is in any runner's tank, and if it isn't replenished between workouts that reservoir will soon be empty. While it is a worthwhile training experience to overstress your system to run off "fumes," that should be a rare exception rather than the rule. Depriving the body of proper recovery and rest is like running without adequate food or drink; eventually breakdown will occur, at which point you'll have to stop longer than you would had you worked adequate recovery and rest periods into your training schedule.

To assure that easy days or recovery runs are not overly strenuous, arrange to run with someone who is willing to run at a moderate pace. Avoid running with someone who has a proclivity to pick it up, or with whom you tend to be competitive. Consider running without a watch, or wear a heart rate monitor that can be set to warn if a predetermined rate is exceeded. Be open to the idea of walking ascents, stopping to stretch, or simply smelling the flowers and enjoying a vista.

A trail runner may boast of having put in a solid month of 120-mile weeks, yet show little to no benefit from such high mileage. Alternatively, a runner who puts in as little as 30-40 miles a week in three or four runs can show tremendous progress if each of those runs serves a particular training purpose. Design the easy days to accomplish a purpose, and transfer any pent-up energy to the hard or long days, to really make those workouts count toward improvement.

Although trail running may not beat up a trail runner the way road or track running does, it is still important to incorporate recovery and rest into training. Recovery and rest periods should come between repeats and intervals, between hard workouts, and before and after races. The use of recovery and rest also applies on a macro level, such as scheduling a particular season, or year, to build to a specific running goal. A trail runner often picks a race as far off as a year, then trains with that race in mind, perhaps running several "training" races geared to preparing for "the target" race.

The training principle of "periodization" (also called "phase" training) is based on the idea that an athlete may reach a performance peak by building up through a set of steps, each of which may last for weeks or months, depending on the starting point and where the athlete wants to be at the peak of the periodization training. Periodization training starts with a buildup, or foundation period, upon which is built a base of endurance and strength. From there, the athlete works on speed and endurance, incorporating distance, tempo runs, intervals, repeats, and fartleks. Once the fitness and strength levels are sufficient to run the target distance at a pace that is close to the goal, focus is reoriented to speed work and turnover, to tweak muscles for a fast pace. It is at this point that the athlete is ready for a recovery phase, also known as the "taper" period.

Within the big picture of a periodization schedule, you should be prepared to make microadjustments for recovery and rest, to stave off overtraining or injury. Know your body and be aware of heightened heart rate; sleep problems; loss of appetite; tight or sore muscles, bones, and connective tissue; a short temper; a general lack of enthusiasm; or other symptoms of burnout. Get adequate sleep with a consistent sleep routine. Quality of rest is probably more important than quantity, and playing catch-up does not always work to restore your body to a rested state. Also be sure to eat a balanced diet with adequate calories and fluids to power through the workout and the entire day.

Engaging in yoga or meditation can play a useful part in the recovery and rest phase. Just because you are not running trails during time off doesn't mean you must sacrifice the peace of mind gained from running in a beautiful place. Those who practice meditative arts are able to reach a similar state of equanimity and tranquility to that gained by running trails, without lifting a foot. Another restorative measure, if available, is a sauna, hot tub, or steam room. The benefits of sports massage are also likely to be worth the time and cost.

When determining the amount of recovery and rest needed, consider the impact of other life events and the effect that family, work, travel, social, and emotional lives have on training—and vice versa. The need may arise to run more or less during particularly stressful periods, regardless of the specific point in the periodization schedule. If emotionally drained, a long slow run in a scenic environment might replace what was supposed to be a hard hill repeat day.

Know yourself, set reasonable short- and long-term goals, and be willing to adjust them. Be flexible and avoid imposing on yourself a training partner's or someone else's goals. Every trail runner is an individual, and responds to different types of training. What works for one trail runner might be a huge mistake for another.

A holistic approach to trail running will keep training in perspective. Avoiding overtraining or chronic fatigue. Approaching each run with fervor keeps you motivated and assures quality training. You will also run more easily if not burdened with stress or a lack of recovery, rest, and relaxation. Finally, common sense trumps total exhaustion, lasting pain, and serious injury.

Running trails with a sense of purpose and strength is an invigorating experience that cultivates a deep sensation of satisfaction, one that overflows and leads to a fulfilling life.

CASTLEWOOD CANYON STATE PARK

ONE OF COLORADO'S FORTY-TWO STATE PARKS, Castlewood Canyon State Park is located 5 miles south of Franktown and approximately 40 miles north of Colorado Springs. With 2,634 acres and 14 miles of trails, this area begs for exploration. The trails are a mixture of singletrack and wider pathways, technical in spots with exposed tree roots and rocks. There are long flat sections along the creek bed, and gnarly ascents to the upper reaches of the canyon. Trails are mostly well marked, albeit an occasional unmarked junction. Housed within the park's environs are remains of the ill-fated Castlewood Dam, which burst on August 3, 1933, sending water cascading to Denver and causing major flooding in the city. Another piece of history is realized in the Lucas Homestead on the west end of the park. Consider a self-guided tour of the homestead remains during a visit to the park.

6-MILE LAKE GULCH/RIMROCK LOOP

THE RUN DOWN

START: Canyon Point parking area; elevation 6,178 feet

OVERALL DISTANCE: 6.3-mile loop

APPROXIMATE RUNNING TIME: 80 minutes

DIFFICULTY: Blue

ELEVATION GAIN: 636 feet

BEST SEASON TO RUN: Year-round

DOG FRIENDLY: Leashed dogs permitted on designated trails

PARKING: A day-use fee is charged; an annual pass is available

OTHER USERS: Equestrians and mountain bikers on designated trails

CELL PHONE COVERAGE: Good

MORE INFORMATION: http://cpw.state.co.us/placestogo/parks/CastlewoodCanyon/Documents/Castlewood-StateParkMap.pdf

FINDING THE TRAILHEAD

Enter the park at the southeast end, located off CO 83, and continue past the toll booth to the second parking area, Canyon Point. The trailhead for the Lake Gulch Trail is on the north side of the parking lot just beyond the interpretive signs and restrooms.

RUN DESCRIPTION

Start on the sidewalk and connect to the singletrack terrain of the Lake Gulch Trail. Pass the amphitheater on the left and continue winding down to the canyon floor. Meet up with the Creek Bottom Trail, which includes well-placed boulders to cross Cherry Creek. The trail is rocky in spots, mostly singletrack, and provides wonderful canyon vistas.

Continue to the Cherry Creek Trail, passing the west-side trail parking lot, and follow the trail north to the Homestead Trail. Head south and look for the self-guided, numbered signage for the Lucas Homestead. Follow #4 to join the Rimrock Trail.

This is the steepest part of this clockwise loop. Climb, climb, and climb some more to the canyon ridge where you can continue south for an out-and-back trek to enjoy vistas, before turning back down the canyon to meet up with the Dam Trail, which takes you back to the Lake Gulch Trail and the starting point in the parking lot.

2-MILE CASTLEWOOD LOOP

THE RUN DOWN

START: Inner Canyon trailhead in the Canyon Point parking lot; elevation 6,603 feet

OVERALL DISTANCE: 1.8-mile loop

APPROXIMATE RUNNING TIME: 25 minutes

DIFFICULTY: Blue

ELEVATION GAIN: 201 feet

BEST SEASON TO RUN: Year-Round, but watch for rattlesnakes in the warmer months and icy patches after winter storms

DOG FRIENDLY: Leashed dogs permitted on designated trails

PARKING: A day-use fee is charged; an annual pass is available

OTHER USERS: Equestrians and mountain bikers on designated trails

CELL PHONE COVERAGE: Good

MORE INFORMATION: http://cpw.state.co.us/placestogo/parks/CastlewoodCanyon/Documents/Castlewood-StateParkMap.pdf

FINDING THE TRAILHEAD

Enter the park at the southeast end, located off CO 83, and continue past the toll booth to the second parking area, Canyon Point. From the Canyon Point parking lot, look for the Inner Canyon trail signage on the sidewalk at the west end of the lot. Continue west on the sidewalk to the trailhead.

RUN DESCRIPTION

This short loop can be repeated in a clockwise or counterclockwise direction for additional mileage. Consider that trails look different when run in reverse direction, thus providing an entirely new look to the route.

The route is described counterclockwise. Be prepared to descend from the outset; no warm-up on flat terrain. Head down switchbacks and a series of steps to the canyon floor. Cross a footbridge over Cherry Creek, and continue on singletrack with rather technical, rocky footing. Enjoy running alongside the creek, crossing a footbridge along the way. After about 1 mile, cross back over the creek on well-positioned boulders to connect with the Lake Gulch Trail for a climb back up the canyon to the parking lot.

ROXBOROUGH STATE PARK

THE BEAUTY OF THIS NEARLY 4,000-ACRE PARK IS EVIDENCED in the naturally sculpted red sandstone formations reputed to be over 300 million years old. The rocks jut from the ground at a 60-degree angle, providing magnificent photo opportunities from the floor of the park as well as from vantage points on the trails at the upper reaches of the park. Without a doubt, this park is awe-inspiring, and definitely worth a visit.

Trails are very well signed and expertly constructed; the majority are singletrack. The park was established in 1975 and abuts Pike National Forest to the west and open space to the east. Nelson Ranch Open Space, a 695-acre parcel, is southeast of the park and is accessed by the Swallowtail Trail. This trail also connects to the 4.6-mile Sharptail Trail, which leads northeast to the Sharptail Ridge Open Space.

CARPENTER PEAK OUT-AND-BACK

THE RUN DOWN

START: Trailhead at the visitor center; elevation 6,205 feet

OVERALL DISTANCE: 6.7 miles

APPROXIMATE RUNNING TIME: 75 minutes

DIFFICULTY: Blue

ELEVATION GAIN: 1,154 feet

BEST SEASON TO RUN: Summer and fall

DOG FRIENDLY: No dogs allowed

PARKING: Free

OTHER USERS: None

CELL PHONE COVERAGE: Good

MORE INFORMATION: http://cpw.state.co.us/placestogo/parks/Roxborough

FINDING THE TRAILHEAD

From I-25, take exit 184 for Sedalia/US 85. Head west on Founders Parkway, traveling 11 miles to Titan Parkway. Turn left and continue along Rampart Range Road. After about 4 miles turn left on North Roxborough Road, and then right on East Roxborough Road. Follow East Roxborough Road for 2 miles to the visitor center. The trail starts across from the visitor center on a wide dirt path.

RUN DESCRIPTION

Follow the smooth, slightly uphill, doubletrack trail to a junction with the South Rim Trail. Continue on the Carpenter Peak Trail which, for the remainder of the climb, is singletrack complete with switchbacks leading uphill to numerous scenic vistas. Views of the red sandstone below are reminiscent of similar scenery found at Colorado Springs' Garden of the Gods Park. Sections of the trail are within shaded forest, while other portions are bordered on both sides by sometimes overgrown scrub oak, which hides rooted and rocky terrain underfoot. Focus is essential to avoid a fall.

Although most of the 3.2-mile route to Carpenter Peak is uphill, there are sections of gentle rolling terrain where you can stretch your legs and gain momentum before the next section of climbing. In the last push to the summit, the trail narrows and becomes rocky. Once at the summit, the views include Mounts Evans and Bierstadt, Waterton Canyon (a stop along the Colorado Trail) and, of course, the red sandstone on the valley floor.

On the return trip, be mindful of the footing as you most likely travel at a faster pace on the descent. Stop to enjoy the views, or take an extra contemplative moment at one of the park benches located at viewpoints slightly off the trail. For a change of scenery near the end of this out-and-back, choose either the 3-mile South Rim Loop Trail, or the 1.4-mile Willow Creek Loop Trail, both signed at junctions. The latter is included on this route. The trail heads a bit east, and crosses a few footbridges before turning back north and west to the visitor center.

COLORADO SPRINGS RUNS

BEAR CREEK REGIONAL PARK

IN THE EL PASO COUNTY PARK SYSTEM, the 545-acre Bear Creek Regional Park offers 11 miles of multiuse trails covering two areas—Bear Creek East and Bear Creek West—separated by 21st Street. There is a streetlight at 21st Street and West Rio Grande Street for a safe road crossing. Additional recreation opportunities in the park include a fenced off-leash dog park, an archery range, playgrounds, picnic facilities, and a community garden. Trails in Bear Creek West can be accessed from Bear Creek Nature Center to the north, or from 21st Street and Argus Boulevard to the south. Bear Creek East can be easily accessed from trailheads located south off West Rio Grande Street.

EAST SIDE OF PARK REPEATED 4K LOOP

THE RUN DOWN

START: Elevation 6,100 feet

OVERALL DISTANCE: 7.5-mile loop

APPROXIMATE RUNNING TIME: 70 minutes

DIFFICULTY: Green

ELEVATION GAIN: 477 feet

BEST SEASON TO RUN: Year-round

DOG FRIENDLY: Leashed dogs permitted

PARKING: Free

OTHER USERS: Equestrians, mountain bikers

CELL PHONE COVERAGE: Good

MORE INFORMATION:
http://adm.elpasoco.com/CommunityServices/ParkOperations/Pages/BearCreekRegionalPark.aspx

FINDING THE TRAILHEAD

From Interstate 25, take exit 141 and continue west on US Highway 24 to 21st Street. Turn south on 21st Street to West Rio Grand Avenue and head east following signage to the park. There is ample parking in the lots, one of which is located at the administrative offices, the other by the community garden. From the parking lot at the administrative offices for Bear Creek Park, cross the small footbridge at the north end of the lot and head north to the gazebo. Start the run heading east on wide path.

RUN DESCRIPTION

Starting on the wide dirt and gravel path, head east across the paved road to connect with the doubletrack trail on the other side of the road. Dip down across a footbridge to head south, then east through a wooded area. Cross over a second footbridge before emerging from the woods to the open meadows in the park. Follow the outer trail east for a wide sweeping perimeter loop on a primarily wide, smooth path with rolling hills, as well as a long ascent to the high point on the south side of the park. The views—the foothills of Pikes Peak and the city of Colorado Springs among them—are worth the climb, and the long descent along the west side of the park is equally enjoyable. Follow the trail back to the junction located just beyond the parking lot on the north side of the community garden, and repeat the loop two more times for a quality 12-kilometer workout.

WEST SIDE OF PARK 4-MILER

THE RUN DOWN

START: Trailhead is located just north of the large gazebo; elevation 6,176 feet

OVERALL DISTANCE: 4.2 miles

APPROXIMATE RUNNING TIME: 45 minutes

DIFFICULTY: Green

ELEVATION GAIN: 560 feet

BEST SEASON TO RUN: Year-round

DOG FRIENDLY: Leashed dogs permitted

PARKING: Free

OTHER USERS: Equestrians, mountain bikers

CELL PHONE COVERAGE: Good

MORE INFORMATION: http://adm.elpasoco.com/CommunityServices/ParkOperations/Pages/BearCreekRegionalPark.aspx

FINDING THE TRAILHEAD

From 21st Street, turn west on Argus Boulevard and park in the lot near the pavilion, just west of the restrooms. The Bear Creek Regional Trail starts at the north end of the parking lot on a wide dirt and gravel path. This is a very well-signed route with maps at several of the junctions to help in route navigation.

RUN DESCRIPTION

Follow the Regional Trail, a doubletrack, smooth-surfaced, rolling and winding trail, about a mile-and-a-half to the Bear Creek Nature Center. Most of this section is in open meadows, although there is partial shade from the trees flanking the far north and west sections of the trail leading to the nature center.

Follow the trail to the front of the nature center, where a short section of sidewalk leads to a junction. Take the singletrack trail to the west and cross a footbridge. For the next mile-and-a-half, enjoy singletrack trail. Follow the creek (on the right), and ascend several sections of water bars and steps to reach the Coyote Gulch Trail.

This trail also has a connection that leads to Section 16, another trail featured in this guide. Loop around this singletrack to connect with the Mountain Scrub Trail, another singletrack and the only section on this route with technical footing. Follow to the junction with the wider Regional Trail, and return on this keyhole, counterclockwise route to the start point.

As much of this route is in the open, enjoy vistas that include Cheyenne Mountain to the south, the foothills to the west, the city of Colorado Springs and Bear Creek East trails to the east, and an occasional glimpse of the rocky outcroppings featured in the Garden of the Gods Park to the north.

FOX RUN REGIONAL PARK

THIS 417-ACRE PARK SITS IN THE NORTHEAST QUADRANT of Colorado Springs, and offers several access points to more than 4 miles of trails. In addition to the trail network, there are two ponds, playgrounds, picnic facilities, and a dog park, making Fox Run the most visited of the nine parks in the El Paso County parks system. In the winter months, the trails are wide enough to enjoy cross-country skiing.

PERIMETER LOOP

THE RUN DOWN

START: Fox Run Regional Park trailhead; elevation 7,500 feet

OVERALL DISTANCE: 3.1-mile loop

APPROXIMATE RUNNING TIME: 35 minutes

DIFFICULTY: Green

ELEVATION GAIN: 322 feet

BEST SEASON TO RUN: Year-round

DOG FRIENDLY: Leashed dogs permitted

PARKING: Free

OTHER USERS: Equestrians. mountain Bikers

CELL PHONE COVERAGE: Fair

MORE INFORMATION:
http://adm.elpasoco.
com/CommunityServices/
ParkOperations/Pages/
FoxRunRegionalPark.aspx

FINDING THE TRAILHEAD

From I-25, take the North Gate Boulevard exit and head east to Roller Coaster Road. (If coming north on CO 83, turn left onto North Gate Boulevard, and right on Roller Coaster Road.) Follow Roller Coaster Road north to the trailhead parking lot on the west side of the road. The trail is just a few feet from the restroom facility located on the east side of the parking lot.

RUN DESCRIPTION

This perimeter loop is run in a counterclockwise direction starting on the northernmost of the three trails adjacent to the restroom. After a short half-mile climb, the trail is gently rolling, but mostly downhill until the 2-mile mark. The final mile has a climb back to the start point. Trails are wide and smooth with an occasional tree root and exposed rock. For much of the route, follow small blue markings on trees, but be advised that junctions are not well signed. This route provides a good overview of the park, but misses the trails around the pond.

LOOPED ROUTE WITH A FINISH ON THE ROAD

THE RUN DOWN

START: Elevation 7,500 feet

OVERALL DISTANCE: 7.0-mile loop

APPROXIMATE RUNNING TIME: 70 minutes

DIFFICULTY: Blue

ELEVATION GAIN: 934 feet

BEST SEASON TO RUN: Spring, summer, fall

DOG FRIENDLY: Leashed dogs permitted

PARKING: Free

OTHER USERS: Equestrians and mountain bikers on designated trails (foot traffic only around the ponds)

CELL PHONE COVERAGE: Fair

MORE INFORMATION: http://adm.elpasoco.com/CommunityServices/ParkOperations/Pages/FoxRunRegionalPark.aspx

FINDING THE TRAILHEAD

From I-25, take the North Gate Boulevard exit and head east to Roller Coaster Road. (If coming north on CO 83, turn left onto North Gate Boulevard, and right on Roller Coaster Road.) Follow Roller Coaster Road north to the trailhead parking lot on the west side of the road. The trail is just a few feet from the restroom facility located on the east side of the parking lot.

RUN DESCRIPTION

This route encompasses most of the park's trails, including some interior loops for added distance. Trails are mostly wide, smooth paths with some decent climbs affording glimpses of Pikes Peak in the distance. The majority of the route is treed, which blocks the wind and promises a serene and peaceful experience. Beyond the views of the peak, the highlight of the park is the pond, complete with a seasonal fountain.

Although most junctions are not marked, there are park benches where you can pause to contemplate your route and stop to study a map of the area. Interpretive signs are scattered throughout the trails should you be interested in learning about the local flora. There are a few points on this route when the trail reaches the dirt road, which runs through the interior of the park. The trail then picks up on the other side of the road for a continuation of the trail journey. After circling the pond, this route includes a section on the dirt road that meets the paved Roller Coaster Road heading north for approximately 1 mile back to the trailhead parking lot.

GARDEN OF THE GODS PARK

GARDEN OF THE GODS, A CITY PARK, is one of the most popular tourist attractions in Colorado Springs. Famous for its prehistoric rock formations, this city park boasts 15 miles of trails, most of which are short, 0.5-mile to 1.0-mile sections joined together for a navigable 4.0-mile route around the perimeter of the park. In addition to the perimeter route, numerous trails crisscross the interior of the park, and some also lead to the gravel Rampart Range Road, which heads some 60 miles north to end at CO 67 between Sedalia and Deckers.

The trails in the park are, in a word, glorious. The scenery is outstanding. The Kissing Camels rock formation is prevalent for much of the route, and the picture-window view of Pikes Peak through the Siamese Twins aperture is a highlight of the park.

Garden of the Gods is a special spot no matter where you are on the trails.
PHOTO BY NANCY HOBBS

GARDEN OF THE GODS PARK

THE RUN DOWN

START: Elevation 6,474 feet

OVERALL DISTANCE: 5.7-mile loop

APPROXIMATE RUNNING TIME: 1 hour

DIFFICULTY: Blue

ELEVATION GAIN: 764 feet

BEST SEASON TO RUN: Year-round

DOG FRIENDLY: Dogs must be on leash at all times

PARKING: Free

OTHER USERS: Multiuse; equestrians and mountain bikers on designated trails

CELL PHONE COVERAGE: Yes

MORE INFORMATION: www.gardenofthegods.com

FINDING THE TRAILHEAD

Park at the main lot accessed via Gateway Drive from 30th Street. The parking lot is located at the northernmost point in the park, where there are toilet facilities and drinking water.

RUN DESCRIPTION

To start the perimeter loop, cross the street and head north on the single-track trail to a signpost for the Palmer Trail. Heading in a counterclock-wise direction, follow the Palmer Trail west, and at most junctions bear to the westernmost fork. Trail markers help guide the way, with signposts for connections to the Siamese Twins, Cabin Canyon, Buckskin Charley, Niobrara, and Chambers. At the east side of the park, the Susan G. Bretag Trail is the final connector to complete the loop.

Well maintained, but with a rustic outdoor feel, the primarily single-track trail includes a mix of rocky steps, smooth and sandy footing, tree roots, navigable boulders, and water bars for erosion control. Plenty of rolling terrain provides a challenge, and totals nearly 700 feet of elevation change in the featured 5.7-mile loop.

Stop in at the Trading Post or the Garden of the Gods Visitor Center to enjoy a light repast, or pick up a trinket or two in the gift shop.

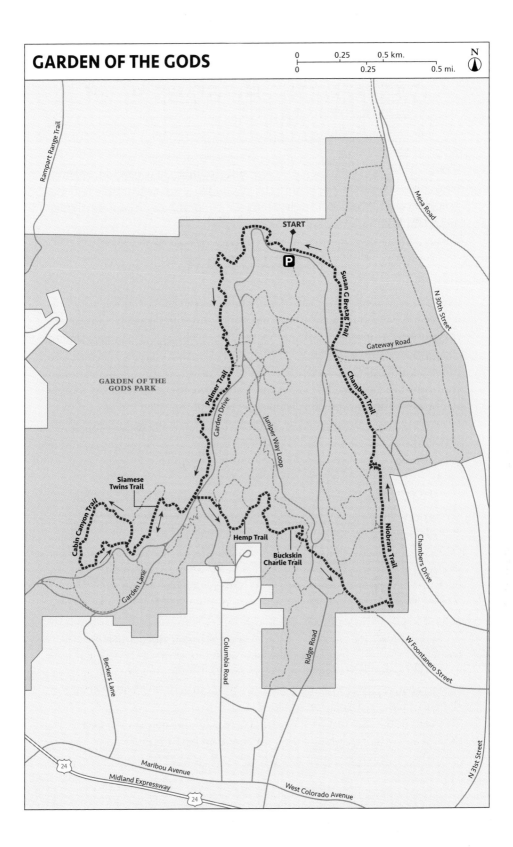

GARDEN OF THE GODS

0   0.25   0.5 km.

0   0.25   0.5 mi.

N

Rampart Range Trail

Mesa Road

N 30th Street

START

P

Susan C Bretag Trail

Gateway Road

GARDEN OF THE
GODS PARK

Palmer Trail

Garden Drive

Chambers Trail

Juniper Way Loop

Siamese
Twins Trail

Cabin Canyon Trail

Chambers Drive

Hemp Trail

Buckskin
Charlie Trail

Niobrara Trail

Garden Lane

Columbia Road

Ridge Road

W Foontanero Street

Beckers Lane

N 31st Street

24

Maribou Avenue

Midland Expressway

24

West Colorado Avenue

PALMER PARK

NAMED FOR WILLIAM JACKSON PALMER, founder of Colorado Springs, whose estate donated the land to the city in 1907, this urban park is a true gem with over 25 miles of trails often used by local race promoters to stage mountain bike and running races.

MESA TRAIL

One of the reasons to run the Mesa Trail is its off-leash, dog-friendly policy. Beyond the ability to enjoy time with your unrestrained four-pawed companions, this is an ideal candidate for beginning trail runners due to the gentle terrain, with less than 100 feet of elevation change. The trail also provides multiple access points to more technical routes for the seasoned trail-running veteran. The sweeping vista of the Pikes Peak massif, visible to the west throughout the 2-plus mile loop, along with views of downtown Colorado Springs and the Garden of the Gods in the distance, make this a spectacular spot.

THE RUN DOWN

START: Ute Crest parking lot; elevation 6,560 feet

OVERALL DISTANCE: 2.3-mile keyhole

APPROXIMATE RUNNING TIME: 35 minutes

DIFFICULTY: Green

ELEVATION GAIN: 92 feet

BEST SEASON TO RUN: Year-round; the trail gets a lot of sun

DOG FRIENDLY: Dogs may run off-leash

PARKING: Free

OTHER USERS: Multiuse; mountain bikers, dog walkers, equestrians

CELL PHONE COVERAGE: Yes

MORE INFORMATION: https://coloradosprings.gov/sites/default/files/parks_recreation_and_cultural_services/parks/palmer_park_map_page_1_of_2.pdf

Pikes Peak is visible on much of the western section of the trails in Palmer Park.
PHOTO BY NANCY HOBBS

FINDING THE TRAILHEAD

Like the Mesa Trail, there are many other trailheads in the park accessible by car. To reach the Mesa Trail, enter the park at either the Maizeland Road entrance to the south, or from North Circle Drive to the west. Follow the main roadway through the park—Paseo Road—to the gravel road junction marked with signage to Ute Crest and Lazy Land. Head northwest and stay on the upper section of the road until it ends at the parking lot.

RUN DESCRIPTION

The Mesa Trail is signed in several spots with trail markers affixed to the top of well-positioned upright posts. The trail is wide, gravel-strewn, and unlike many of the other singletrack trail options—which aren't marked quite as well at forks and junctures—is easy to follow.

TEMPLETON TRAIL

THE RUN DOWN

START: Ute Crest parking lot; elevation 6,548 feet

OVERALL DISTANCE: 3.9-mile loop

APPROXIMATE RUNNING TIME: 50 minutes

DIFFICULTY: Blue

ELEVATION GAIN: 523 feet

BEST SEASON TO RUN: Year-round; avoid during heavy rain or snow

DOG FRIENDLY: Dogs must be on leash at all times

PARKING: Free

OTHER USERS: Multiuse; mountain bikers, equestrians

CELL PHONE COVERAGE: Yes

MORE INFORMATION: https://coloradosprings.gov/sites/default/files/parks_recreation_and_cultural_services/parks/palmer_park_map_page_1_of_2.pdf

FINDING THE TRAILHEAD

Like the Mesa Trail, there are many other trailheads in the park accessible by car. To reach the Mesa Trail, enter the park at either the Maizeland Road entrance to the south, or from North Circle Drive to the west. Follow the main roadway through the park—Paseo Road—to the gravel road junction marked with signage to Ute Crest and Lazy Land. Head northwest and stay on the upper section of the road until it ends at the parking lot.

RUN DESCRIPTION

The more technical Templeton Trail can be accessed at many points in the park, including the Mesa Trail. This 4-mile route is easiest to follow in a clockwise direction from a starting point near the Ute Crest parking area. Look for the yellow trail sign and go south a few hundred feet on single-track to an upright post signed Templeton Trail and the foreboding black diamond designation most familiar to downhill skiers.

The trail does not disappoint those seeking a challenge. Very technical rocky sections, requiring focus and navigation, are located throughout the 4-mile loop. Likewise, there are smooth sections of flat or rolling terrain all

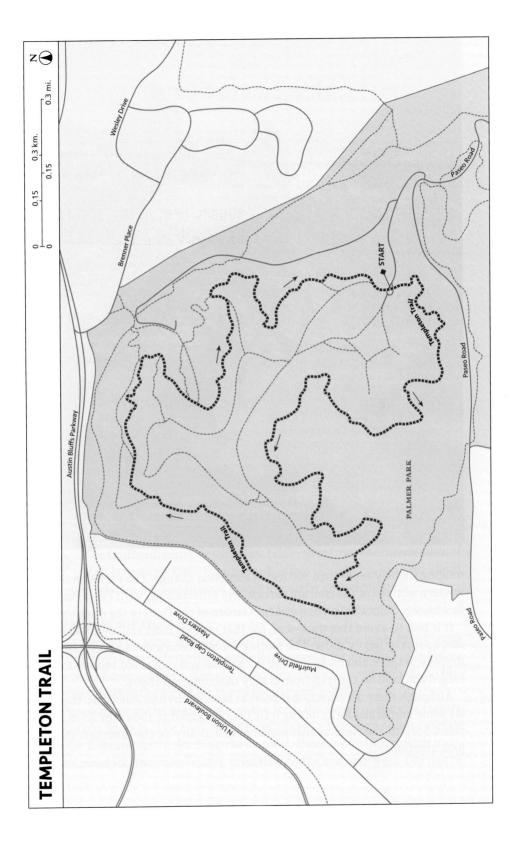

TEMPLETON TRAIL

START

Templeton Trail

Templeton Trail

PALMER PARK

Austin Bluffs Parkway

N Union Boulevard

Templeton Gap Road

Masters Drive

Muirfield Drive

Paseo Road

Paseo Road

Wesley Drive

Brenner Place

N

| 0 | 0.15 | 0.3 km. |

| 0 | 0.15 | 0.3 mi. |

SECTION 16/PALMER LOOP

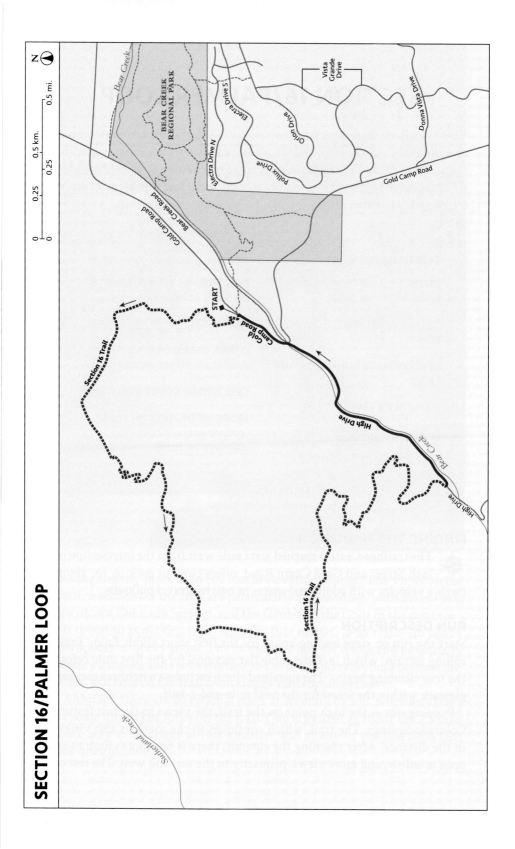

Flowing singletrack on the
Section 16/Palmer Loop.
PHOTO BY NANCY HOBBS

the loop is mostly downhill, or rolling in nature, and includes a short creek crossing after the 3.0-mile point.

There are a few questionable and unmarked forks. At any and all junctures, stay left, including at the final turn out of the forest onto a gravel roadway; this is High Drive, which intersects with Gold Camp Road after about 1 mile of downhill running back (north) toward the trailhead. Turning right on High Drive leads uphill to Cheyenne Cañon and an abundance of trails, some of which are featured in this guide.

Additional mileage can also be realized from several access points in the first mile of the Section 16 route. Watch for signs to the Intemann Trail, linking the route to Red Rock Canyon Open Space. In 2003, the city purchased this incredible 789-acre open space, which now offers nearly 16 miles of trails, some of which lead to Manitou Springs.

RED ROCK CANYON OPEN SPACE

THE CITY OF COLORADO SPRINGS PURCHASED THIS 789-ACRE PARCEL located between Colorado Springs and Manitou Springs in 2003. Recreation opportunities abound, including climbing (with permit), hiking, mountain biking, horseback riding, and picnicking. There is a freeride bike course, as well as an off-leash dog park. With more than 12 miles of well-signed trails, this area is complete with a pond, rock quarries, ridges, canyons, ascents and descents, all amid diverse terrain, making it a true gem in the Pikes Peak region.

3-MILE LOOP

THE RUN DOWN

START: Mesa Trail; elevation 6,194 feet

OVERALL DISTANCE: 3.0-mile loop

APPROXIMATE RUNNING TIME: 35 minutes

DIFFICULTY: Green

ELEVATION GAIN: 498 feet

BEST SEASON TO RUN: Year-round

DOG FRIENDLY: Leashed dogs permitted

PARKING: Free

OTHER USERS: Equestrians and mountain bikers on designated trails

CELL PHONE COVERAGE: Fair

MORE INFORMATION: http://redrockcanyonopenspace.org/

FINDING THE TRAILHEAD

Red Rock Canyon is located on US 24, just west of 31st Street off Ridge Road, approximately 4 miles west of downtown Colorado Springs and 2 miles east of Manitou Springs. The start point for this route is the Mesa Trail, located at the center of the park on the south side of the parking lot.

RUN DESCRIPTION

Follow the Mesa Trail, a double-wide red dirt trail, on a mostly uphill trajectory to the high point on this route. Enjoy stunning views of the Garden of the Gods to the north, Colorado Springs to the east, and an occasional glimpse of Pikes Peak to the west.

At the end of the Mesa Trail, take a short singletrack section of technical downhill to the base of the canyon. Meet up with the Red Rock Canyon Trail and head north, past the pond and through an access gate, and then turn just before the east parking lot to return to the start point. This route is well signed and maps are located at various points in the park to assist with navigation.

10K KEYHOLE LOOP WITH OUT-AND-BACK

THE RUN DOWN

START: Contemplative Trail; elevation 6,207 feet

OVERALL DISTANCE: 6.1 miles round-trip

APPROXIMATE RUNNING TIME: 75 minutes

DIFFICULTY: Blue

ELEVATION GAIN: 1,160 feet

BEST SEASON TO RUN: Year-round

DOG FRIENDLY: Leashed dogs permitted

PARKING: Free

OTHER USERS: Equestrians and mountain bikers on designated trails

CELL PHONE COVERAGE: Fair

MORE INFORMATION: http://redrockcanyonopenspace.org/

FINDING THE TRAILHEAD

Red Rock Canyon is located on US 24, just west of 31st Street off Ridge Road, approximately 4 miles west of downtown Colorado Springs and 2 miles east of Manitou Springs. Start at the trailhead located at the southwest end of the parking lot off US 24, on the trail farthest west from the parking lot, signed Contemplative Trail.

RUN DESCRIPTION

Head south on the Contemplative Trail, past rocky outcroppings in partial shade. The trail has several sections of steps on singletrack terrain. Follow to the singletrack Roundup Trail and continue south, winding around tight turns to the east to reach the Mesa Trail (this trail is featured in the 3-mile route). Turn right again, heading south. Follow the wider and smoother Mesa Trail for about 0.5 mile to the first major singletrack trail on the right. Head south through the meadow to the junction with the (Paul) Intemann (Memorial Nature) Trail, a rambling, often-technical singletrack trail, and follow that west to a creek crossing.

Continue over the footbridge to the paved road. For this keyhole out-and-back route, return to the Intemann signage and turn north on the Sand Canyon Trail. (Should you desire a longer effort, cross the paved road and continue on the Intemann Trail as far as Manitou Springs, or turn around at any point for an out-and-back route.) Follow this singletrack trail, which features numerous switchbacks as it descends to the canyon floor below. Turn left at the Contemplative Trail sign, and return to the starting point.

This route has it all. Singletrack, doubletrack, narrow sections, rock features, shaded sections, technical terrain, and vistas. Spot the Garden of the Gods to the north, downtown Colorado Springs to the east, and Pikes Peak to the west. This route also provides connections to Section 16, the Iron Mountain Trail, and North Cheyenne Cañon, all featured in this guide.

NORTH CHEYENNE CAÑON PARK

ONE OF COLORADO SPRINGS' CITY PARKS, North Cheyenne Cañon provides all that makes Colorado spectacular, with sweeping vistas of the surrounding mountains and valleys, forested pathways, bubbling creeks, waterfalls, and trails to enjoy.

COLUMBINE TRAIL/ SPRING CREEK TRAIL LOOP

THE RUN DOWN

START: Behind the Starsmore Visitor and Nature Center; elevation 6,273 feet

OVERALL DISTANCE: 6.2-mile loop

APPROXIMATE RUNNING TIME: 1.5 hours

DIFFICULTY: Blue

ELEVATION GAIN: 1,233 feet

BEST SEASON TO RUN: Year-round; icy in spots in winter

DOG FRIENDLY: Dogs must be on leash at all times

PARKING: Free

OTHER USERS: Multiuse; few equestrians

CELL PHONE COVERAGE: Yes

MORE INFORMATION: www .cheyennecanon.org

FINDING THE TRAILHEAD

Park at the Starsmore Visitor and Nature Center lot, located at the intersection of North and South Cheyenne Cañon Roads. Head west across the street and follow the sidewalk behind the visitor center to the trailhead marked Lower Columbine Trail.

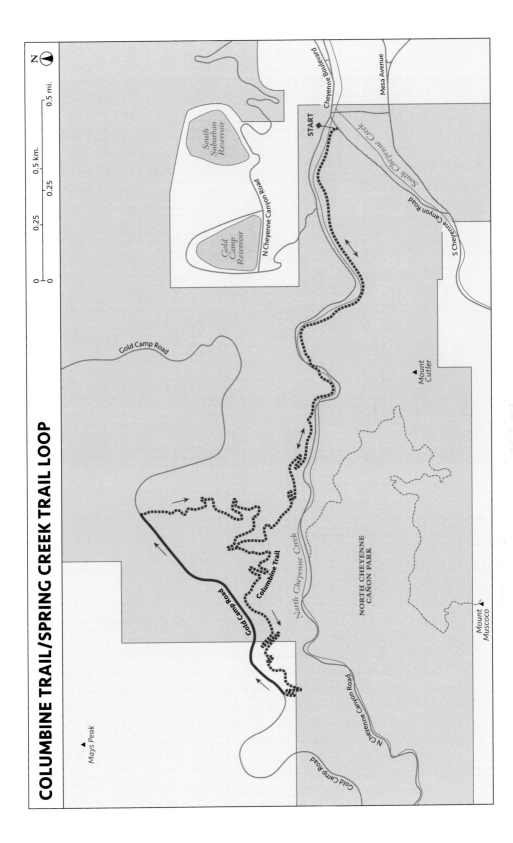

COLUMBINE TRAIL/SPRING CREEK TRAIL LOOP

N

0   0.25   0.5 km.
0   0.25   0.5 mi.

START

Cheyenne Boulevard

Mesa Avenue

South Cheyenne Creek

S Cheyenne Canyon Road

Mount Cutler

South Suburban Reservoir

Gold Camp Reservoir

N Cheyenne Canyon Road

Gold Camp Road

Mays Peak

Gold Camp Road

Columbine Trail

North Cheyenne Creek

NORTH CHEYENNE CAÑON PARK

N Cheyenne Canyon Road

Gold Camp Road

Mount Muscoco

One of the old stone bridges in Cheyenne Cañon connects trails from one side of the park to the other side. PHOTO BY TIM BERGSTEN

RUN DESCRIPTION

Begin on the Lower Columbine Trail proceeding west. When the road comes into view, turn sharply to the left/uphill and follow switchbacks, which will drop down to the road. Cross the road and continue on the singletrack, where the trail becomes steep, with much of the 1,200 feet of climbing encountered in the next mile.

A nice rolling section through forest brings you to a creek crossing. Turn left after crossing the creek and continue uphill. This is the juncture where the Spring Creek Trail meets the Columbine Trail, which is where this keyhole loop converges for the return back to the parking lot.

After the creek crossing, there is more vertical gain, as well as some descending, topping out at a metal sign indicating Gold Camp Road is to the right. Continue to the road and turn right, staying on the gravel road, passing through a tunnel within 1 mile; immediately after the tunnel, turn right onto the Spring Creek Trail, indicated with a sign post.

The rolling Spring Creek Trail, like the Columbine Trail, affords fantastic views of nearby Cheyenne Mountain and rocky outcroppings in the distance. The surface is smooth in spots, rugged and rocky in others, and often laden with scree just to challenge footing and focus.

Within a mile on the Spring Creek Trail, the juncture is reached. Cross the creek to head left back down the Columbine Trail, retracing the route back to the parking lot at the Starsmore visitor center.

In addition to enjoying the exhibits at the center, Seven Falls is another attraction in the area not to be missed. The Cheyenne Mountain Zoo and the Broadmoor Hotel are other spots located nearby, and worthy of a visit—although a meal or shopping at the Broadmoor may quickly shrink your wallet.

MOUNT MUSCOCO

THE RUN DOWN

START: Mount Cutler Trail and Mount Muscoco; 6,722 feet

OVERALL DISTANCE: 4.2 miles out and back

APPROXIMATE RUNNING TIME: 1 hour

DIFFICULTY: Black

ELEVATION GAIN: 1,479 feet

BEST SEASON TO RUN: Year-round; icy in spots in winter

DOG FRIENDLY: Dogs must be on leash at all times

PARKING: Free

OTHER USERS: Multiuse; few equestrians

CELL PHONE COVERAGE: Yes; can be spotty

MORE INFORMATION: www.cheyennecanon.org

FINDING THE TRAILHEAD

The trailhead is reached by heading west from the Starsmore Visitor and Nature Center up North Cheyenne Cañon Road for approximately 1.5 miles. Signage indicates Mount Cutler and Mount Muscoco at a small pullout on the south side of the road.

RUN DESCRIPTION

Another trail to enjoy in Cheyenne Cañon affords access to the highest point in the Colorado Springs city park system, the 8,020-foot summit of Mount Muscoco.

Although the 1-mile out-and-back Mount Cutler Trail has been a mainstay in the park for years, the Mount Muscoco Trail is relatively new, having opened in early 2015. This 4.2-mile round-trip is another gem, featuring 1,479 feet of climbing.

To reach Mount Muscoco, follow the Mount Cutler Trail for approximately 0.5 mile and turn right at the trail marker for Mount Muscoco. Follow the well-marked trail, which is relatively rolling to start and climbs several sets of steps. After reaching grades upward of 45 percent

MOUNT MUSCOCO

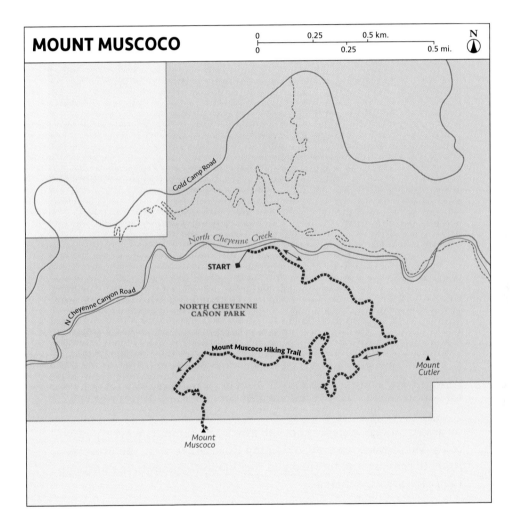

0   0.25   0.5 km.

0   0.25   0.5 mi.

N

Gold Camp Road

North Cheyenne Creek

START

N Cheyenne Canyon Road

NORTH CHEYENNE
CAÑON PARK

Mount Muscoco Hiking Trail

Mount
Cutler

Mount
Muscoco

Switchbacks in Cheyenne Cañon.
PHOTO BY TIM BERGSTEN

over very rocky terrain, you will reach the summit, where you will enjoy 360-degree views of Gold Camp Road to the west, the Broadmoor Hotel to the east, and forested and rocky outcroppings to the north and south. Return as you came.

11-MILE LOOP IN THE CAÑON

THE RUN DOWN

START: Starsmore Visitor and Nature Center; elevation 6,274 feet

OVERALL DISTANCE: 11.0-mile loop

APPROXIMATE RUNNING TIME: 110 minutes

DIFFICULTY: Blue

ELEVATION GAIN: 2,189 feet

BEST SEASON TO RUN: Springtime for the wildflowers

DOG FRIENDLY: Leashed dogs permitted

PARKING: Free

OTHER USERS: Equestrians and mountain bikers

CELL PHONE COVERAGE: Fair

MORE INFORMATION: https://coloradosprings. gov/parks-recreation-and-cultural-services/page/north-cheyenne-ca%C3%B1on

FINDING THE TRAILHEAD

From the parking lot at the intersection of West Cheyenne Road and South Cheyenne Canyon Road, cross the street and follow the sidewalk to the rear of the Starsmore Visitor and Nature Center, with an address of 2120 South Cheyenne Canyon Road. Start on the singletrack trail accessed through the split rail fence.

RUN DESCRIPTION

After a short climb on singletrack, the path widens as it travels west. Turn left on a section of singletrack and traverse several switchbacks before descending to a stone bridge and crossing the road to pick up the singletrack on the other side. This trail, the Columbine Trail, and the remaining route are well signed.

Follow the Columbine Trail approximately 3 miles to Gold Camp Road, and turn left to reach the upper parking lot at the intersection of High Drive. Turn right up High Drive for about 1 mile to a signpost on the left for the Buckhorn Trail. Follow the trail to an overlook, and return back down the same trail to High Drive, crossing to the east to meet up with

Captain Jack's Trail. More singletrack is in store, with gentle climbing, rolling terrain, and long switchbacks toward the end of the trail, which reaches Gold Camp Road after approximately 2.5 miles.

Turn right and head uphill to the Spring Creek Trail, located on the south side of Gold Camp Road. Enjoy the twists and turns of the Spring Creek Trail, which joins the Columbine Trail after crossing the creek. Follow the trail back to the Starsmore visitor center.

10-MILE LOOP: SEVEN BRIDGES, HIGH DRIVE, AND BUCKHORN

THE RUN DOWN

START: Trailhead on Gold Camp Road; elevation 7,500 feet

OVERALL DISTANCE: 10.0-mile loop

APPROXIMATE RUNNING TIME: 2 hours

DIFFICULTY: Blue

ELEVATION GAIN: 2,808 feet

BEST SEASON TO RUN: Springtime for the wildflowers; fall for the changing colors

DOG FRIENDLY: Leashed dogs permitted

PARKING: Free

OTHER USERS: Equestrians and mountain bikers on designated trails

CELL PHONE COVERAGE: Poor

MORE INFORMATION: https://coloradosprings.gov/parks-recreation-and-cultural-services/page/north-cheyenne-ca%C3%B1on

FINDING THE TRAILHEAD

From South Nevada Avenue, head west on West Cheyenne Road past the intersection of South Cheyenne Canyon Road, and ascend approximately 3 miles up North Cheyenne Cañon to the dirt parking lot at the intersection of High Drive and Gold Camp Road. The start of this route is on the dirt road (Gold Camp Road) just beyond the gate on the west side of the parking lot.

RUN DESCRIPTION

Head west on Gold Camp Road, which is not accessible to cars, approximately 0.7 mile to the trailhead on the right for Seven Bridges (the second junction to the right). Follow this mostly singletrack trail, which travels adjacent to North Cheyenne Creek and is rocky and tree-rooted in sections, over seven bridges (aptly signed with the respective number).

After reaching the final bridge crossing at approximately 2.0 miles, follow Forest Service Trail (FS) #622A, complete with some generous climbing, featuring grades over 20 percent. Along with the climb, there are fantastic views east to the city of Colorado Springs. Follow FS #622A to the junction of FS #667, crossing Bear Creek. Continue downhill, running alongside Bear Creek, until the trail becomes FS #666 and continue downhill. (By staying on FS #667—the trail is also known as the Buckhorn Trail—you will make this route a bit shorter than the advertised 10 miles, and also eliminate a long climb up High Drive).

FS #666 meets High Drive approximately 2.0 miles past the turnoff for Buckhorn Trail. Turn right and run approximately 1.5 miles up High Drive, a wide dirt and gravel road, to the junction of FS #667/Buckhorn Trail on the right. Back on singletrack trail continue climbing, with excellent views of Gold Camp Road below and the Broadmoor Hotel grounds in the distance to the west.

After the initial climb of about 0.75 mile, the trail flattens out. In another quarter-mile, reach a T intersection (this is where the trail would connect as FS #667, mentioned earlier) and turn left. The singletrack trail gradually descends on smooth terrain, albeit with a stray root or rock, with well-placed switchbacks to lessen your speed around the turns. Return to Gold Camp Road where the journey began, and turn left for the 0.7 mile stretch back to the parking lot.

This is a wonderful training run because it offers such a variety of terrain, as well as considerable climbing and descending. The singletrack technical sections require focus, the long climbs require strength and mental toughness, and the long descents require agility and balance. The terrain also includes short sections of scree—ball-bearing-size rocks—that may cause slipping or sliding, especially on the descents. Running alongside the creeks provides melodic timeouts, so forego your headphones not only for safety's sake, but also for the peaceful and musical creek tunes. During the fall, the golden aspens quake, another wonderful sound, and provide excellent photo opportunities.

STRATTON OPEN SPACE

THIS PROPERTY WAS PURCHASED BY THE CITY OF COLORADO SPRINGS IN 1998, with the majority of the funds coming from the Trails Open Space and Parks (TOPS) sales tax. Adjacent to North Cheyenne Cañon, this 317-acre expanse has approximately 6 miles of well-marked trails offering a mixture of single- and doubletrack routes on gently rolling terrain, as well as enjoyable climbing and descending. There are great views of the foothills to the west and glimpses of the Broadmoor Hotel to the south.

4-MILE LOOP

THE RUN DOWN

START: Parking lot off Ridgeway Drive; elevation 6,200 feet

OVERALL DISTANCE: 4.0-mile loop

APPROXIMATE RUNNING TIME: 45 minutes

DIFFICULTY: Blue

ELEVATION GAIN: 755 feet

BEST SEASON TO RUN: Year-round

DOG FRIENDLY: Leashed dogs permitted

PARKING: Free

OTHER USERS: Equestrians and mountain bikers

CELL PHONE COVERAGE: Good

MORE INFORMATION: https://coloradosprings.gov/Stratton

FINDING THE TRAILHEAD

Head west on West Cheyenne Boulevard, crossing Cresta Road, and continue to Ridgeway Drive, which has a sign indicating the parking lot ahead. There is a portable toilet near the trailhead and a limited number of parking spaces. Because there are several access points to the Stratton Open Space, including a parking area on LaVeta Way off Cresta Road, this parking lot is never too crowded.

RUN DESCRIPTION

Run in a counterclockwise loop, this route starts at the trailhead just feet from the parking lot. Start heading north on the Wildflower Path. The trail is singletrack and smooth to start, with minimal climbing, affording the first view corridor within 0.5 mile.

At the top of the first hill, bear left and meet up with the Stratton Springs Path. This is also a singletrack section with some exposed tree roots and rocks, but is not technical. At the Ponderosa Trail sign continue straight, with the reservoir fencing on your left. Take a right at the Chamberlain Trail and continue to the Chutes. Follow the wider Chutes Trail, being mindful of oncoming mountain bikers as this is a favorite downhill route.

Ascend to the Gold Hill Path, designated "no bikes." Follow this winding single- and doubletrack trail, complete with a section of steps, to an open area. Here you can turn left (south) to pick up the Chamberlain Trail, which runs to North Cheyenne Cañon. Continue straight, with the reservoir fencing on your right. This is a wider path, which meets up with a dirt road. Follow the road back to the parking lot.

UTE VALLEY PARK

THIS CITY PARK OFFERS 338 ACRES with a 3.5-mile perimeter trail and interior trails for additional mileage. A mixture of technical trails and smooth, sandy terrain make this a popular destination for mountain bikers and runners. The views are expansive, and the main trails are well signed. The park has hosted numerous trail races, including the annual Blue Moon Trail Race Series to benefit the city of Colorado Springs' community centers.

5K LOOP FROM PIÑON VALLEY PARK

THE RUN DOWN

START: Piñon Valley Park; elevation 6,451 feet

OVERALL DISTANCE: 3.0-mile loop

APPROXIMATE RUNNING TIME: 30 minutes

DIFFICULTY: Blue

ELEVATION GAIN: 321 feet

BEST SEASON TO RUN: Year-round

DOG FRIENDLY: Leashed dogs permitted

PARKING: Free

OTHER USERS: Mountain bikers

CELL PHONE COVERAGE: Good

MORE INFORMATION: https://coloradosprings.gov/parks-recreation-and-cultural-services/page/ute-valley-park

FINDING THE TRAILHEAD

There are several access points to the park, with the main lot on Vindicator Drive just east of Centennial Boulevard. This particular route, however, starts at the southwest side of the park at Piñon Valley Park, which is located east of Centennial Boulevard on Mule Deer Drive.

RUN DESCRIPTION

From the start in Piñon Valley Park, turn right and head up the gravel road for a gut-busting, albeit relatively short—less than a quarter mile—climb. Head west on singletrack, and enjoy quick turns and occasional climbs on rocky and rooted terrain. Stay left at the junctions, reaching the top of the loop near Vindicator Drive. Make a left turn and return on the Ute Valley Park Trail to Piñon Valley Park.

PERIMETER LOOP

THE RUN DOWN

START: South side of the Vindicator Road parking lot; elevation 6,543 feet

OVERALL DISTANCE: 2.5 miles round-trip

APPROXIMATE RUNNING TIME: 25 minutes

DIFFICULTY: Green

ELEVATION GAIN: 284 feet

BEST SEASON TO RUN: Year-Round (be sure to watch for rattlesnakes in the summer).

DOG FRIENDLY: Leashed dogs permitted

PARKING: Free

OTHER USERS: Mountain bikers

CELL PHONE COVERAGE: Good

MORE INFORMATION: https://coloradosprings.gov/parks-recreation-and-cultural-services/page/ute-valley-park

FINDING THE TRAILHEAD

Park at the main lot on Vindicator Road, just west of Eagleview Middle School and east of Centennial Boulevard. The parking lot is on the south side of Vindicator, and there are two trail access points. For this route, follow the trail on the south side of the parking lot.

RUN DESCRIPTION

Starting on a wide pathway signed as Bobcat Cutoff, this route is flat and smooth to start, and transitions to rolling and rocky terrain requiring focus to avoid tripping on loose rock. Connect with the Pine Ridge Trail, cresting a hill and turning east on singletrack, meeting up with Popes Valley Trail. Eventually join with the Yucca Path Trail to complete this counterclockwise loop.

The surfaces vary from loose and sandy to smooth rock, and include double- and singletrack trails. The majority of the route is in the open, with little shade. The views on the upper reaches of the trail are outstanding, and include Pikes Peak and the foothills to the west, and the city of Colorado Springs to the east. Several benches are strategically placed in the park to indicate the most scenic vistas.

CHEYENNE MOUNTAIN STATE PARK

CHEYENNE MOUNTAIN STATE PARK OPENED TO THE PUBLIC IN 2006, and trails are still being added to the nearly 21 miles already in use. One such trail, the Dixon Trail, can be accessed via the North Talon Loop Trail, but will not be opened to the public until its completion slated for 2019. Once completed, the Dixon Trail will climb 3,000 feet over 3 miles to the top of Cheyenne Mountain, and meet up with a planned 3.6-mile route on the summit.

Although there is a fee to access this trail system—it is a state park, after all—it offers 21 miles of trails with rolling terrain, some steep ups and downs, and the opportunity to see lots of wildlife including wild turkeys, foxes, deer, and the occasional rattlesnake and mountain lion. Because of the abundant wildlife and ecosystem, no dogs are allowed on the trails, and horses are permitted only on designated trails.

TALON TRAILS

This route features a mixture of wide paths and flowing singletrack, some within forest, some in open meadows. Some rocky sections and exposed tree roots require focus and agility.

THE RUN DOWN

START: Limekiln day-use trailhead; elevation 6,046 feet

OVERALL DISTANCE: 8 miles

APPROXIMATE RUNNING TIME: Under 2 hours

DIFFICULTY: Green to Blue

ELEVATION GAIN: 1,058 feet

BEST SEASON TO RUN: Year-round; icy in spots in winter, and muddy when wet

DOG FRIENDLY: No dogs permitted on trails, however a pilot program has been launched to consider the viability of leashed dogs on designated trails

PARKING: A day-use fee is charged; an annual pass is available

OTHER USERS: Equestrians on specific sections; mountain bikers

CELL PHONE COVERAGE: Yes

MORE INFORMATION: www .cpw.state.co.us/placestogo/ parks/cheyennemountain

FINDING THE TRAILHEAD

Follow Colorado 115 south from Colorado Springs past the exit for NORAD, turning west (right) at the entrance to Cheyenne Mountain State Park. Follow the access road past the visitor center and toll booth, taking the first left turn into the large parking area. For this tour of the southernmost end of the trail system, start at the Limekiln day-use trailhead, where there is a large parking area and indoor toilet facilities.

RUN DESCRIPTION

From the trailhead, head west across the footbridge to join the Talon Trail. The start of the run is relatively flat, but the route is deceptive at first glance. There are numerous climbs and rolling switchbacks to enjoy along

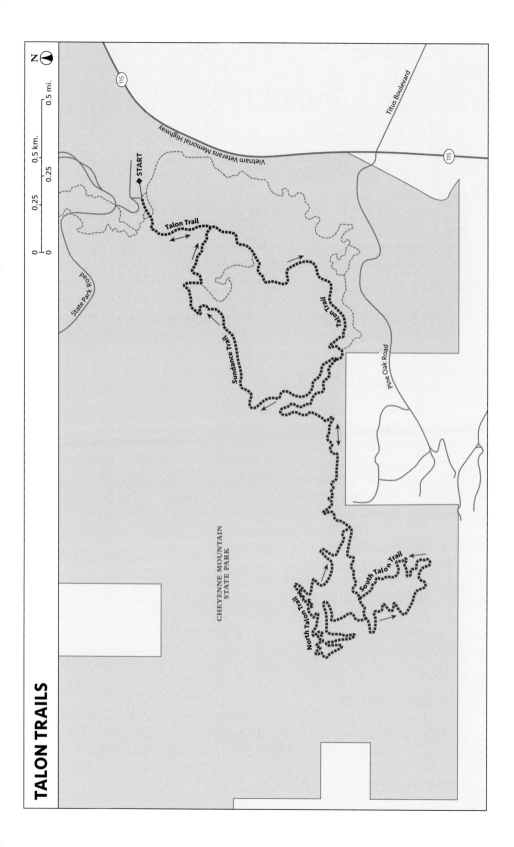

TALON TRAILS

N

0 0.25 0.5 km.

0 0.25 0.5 mi.

115

START

Talon Trail

Talon Trail

Sundance Trail

North Talon Trail

South Talon Trail

CHEYENNE MOUNTAIN
STATE PARK

State Park Road

Pine Oak Road

Vietnam Veterans Memorial Highway

Titus Boulevard

115

Many of the trails in the park have wide sections that allow easy running with several people abreast. PHOTO BY NANCY HOBBS

this route, the first of which is within one half-mile and continues uphill for 2 miles. There are grades upward of 20 percent on the route.

After the footbridge, continue south to reach and run a clockwise loop of the South Talon and North Talon Trails. Return to the Talon Trail and head north toward the trailhead, but turn left (west) on the Sundance Trail to enjoy another trail in the park on the return route. All trails are very well marked, and this trail features a mixture of double- and singletracks with mostly good footing.

It is common to encounter wildlife in the park, from wild turkeys to deer, with an occasional bobcat or mountain lion sighting, although these are less frequent. In the heat, rattlesnakes may sunbathe on the trails. Beware of those in a coiled configuration.

From the trails, enjoy views of the triple-peaked Cheyenne Mountain, which houses none other than NORAD (North American Aerospace Defense Command), built in the Cold War and still fully operational. Within the 1,680-acre park there are campsites and picnic areas, as well as an archery range.

CARING FOR THE TRAIL

WHETHER A TRAIL IS A NEW ADDITION TO AN AREA, a long-established component of a citywide park system, or a remote animal pathway, trail use should be considered a privilege and not a right. As trail users, runners should be respectful of this precious natural resource and do what they can to ensure trails last well into the future. There are numerous advocacy and stewardship programs for the trail runner to consider, and if one doesn't exist in your area, consider starting one to preserve and maintain trails.

Experiencing the natural sights, sounds, smells, and surfaces found on trails is a huge part of the desire to run trails, as opposed to roads. A high density of trails in certain areas detracts from this appeal. Trails have a negative impact on the natural environment they pass though. With a growing population, increased trail use, and recognition that natural areas cannot be all things for all people, trail use may become more restricted in the future. The number and type of trails, and their use, are and will be limited in certain areas to preserve the environment, protect resources, and retain the quality experience all trail users seek. As trails become a limited resource in the future, trail runners will have an advantage because of their flexibility to adapt to all types of trails.

On trails that allow participation by all user groups, cooperation is the key to peaceful coexistence, and it is imperative to ensure the trail will always be around to enjoy. Although each user group enjoys an activity that may be quite different from another's form of recreation, preservation and respect for the environment should be the shared concern of all users. Most users have an advocacy group to turn to for education and support.

The American Trail Running Association (ATRA) promotes the following responsible trail runner tips. compiled by longtime ATRA board member Tom Sobal:

- Stay on marked and existing trails.
- Don't cut switchbacks.
- Go through puddles, not around them.
- Climb or jump over fallen trees instead of going around them.
- When multiple trails exist, run on the one most worn.

- Do not litter, leave no trace, and pack everything out you packed in.
- Use minimum-impact techniques to dispose of human waste.
- Leave what you find—take only photographs.
- Close all gates that you open.
- Keep pets leashed at all times, and be sure to leave pets at home when running in areas posted "no pets."
- Stop to help others in need: Even while racing, sacrifice your event to aid other trail users who might be in trouble.
- Volunteer at trail races—before, during, or after an event.
- Volunteer, support, and encourage others to participate in trail maintenance days.
- Do not disturb or harass wildlife or livestock.
- Stay off closed trails and obey all posted regulations.
- Respect private property; get permission first to go on private land.
- Do not run on muddy or very dusty trails; pick another route so that you don't further damage the trail and cause unnecessary erosion.
- Warn other trail users when passing from behind by calling out "Hello" or "Trail" well in advance to avoid scaring them.
- Know the area you plan to run in and let at least one other person know where you intend to go.
- Dress for the conditions—both existing and potentially changeable.
- Carry plenty of water.
- Be ready to yield to other trail users (bikers, hikers, equestrians).
- Uphill runners yield to downhill runners.
- When preparing to pass a runner, yell "Trail" well in advance.
- Know your limits.

This list has been further refined as a Rules on the Run document available at www.trailrunner.com in a pdf version.

The basis for every outdoor experience rests in safety, appreciation, and environmental awareness. Enjoy trail runs with this in mind.

PALMER LAKE

THE ENCLAVE OF PALMER LAKE, population 2,500, sits north of Colorado Springs. An extensive yet relatively underutilized trail system provides miles of terrain to explore. An enjoyable and very runnable route is the Ice Cave Creek Loop Trail.

ICE CAVE CREEK LOOP TRAIL

THE RUN DOWN

START: Palmer Lake Reservoir trailhead; elevation 7,229 feet

OVERALL DISTANCE: 4.3-mile loop

APPROXIMATE RUNNING TIME: 45 minutes

DIFFICULTY: Blue

ELEVATION GAIN: 1,043 feet

BEST SEASON TO RUN: Late spring, summer, and fall. In early spring the creeks can get a bit deep and icy, and snow remains during the winter months

DOG FRIENDLY: Yes

PARKING: Free

OTHER USERS: No ATVs; bikers, hikers, and equestrian-accessible, though few utilize the area trails

CELL PHONE COVERAGE: Minimal

MORE INFORMATION: http://www.townofpalmerlake.com/

FINDING THE TRAILHEAD

Head west from I-25 north of Colorado Spring on CO 105, and turn left on South Valley Road. In two blocks, turn left on Reservoir Road and follow this to ample parking opportunities. The trailhead is on the westernmost side of the parking lot.

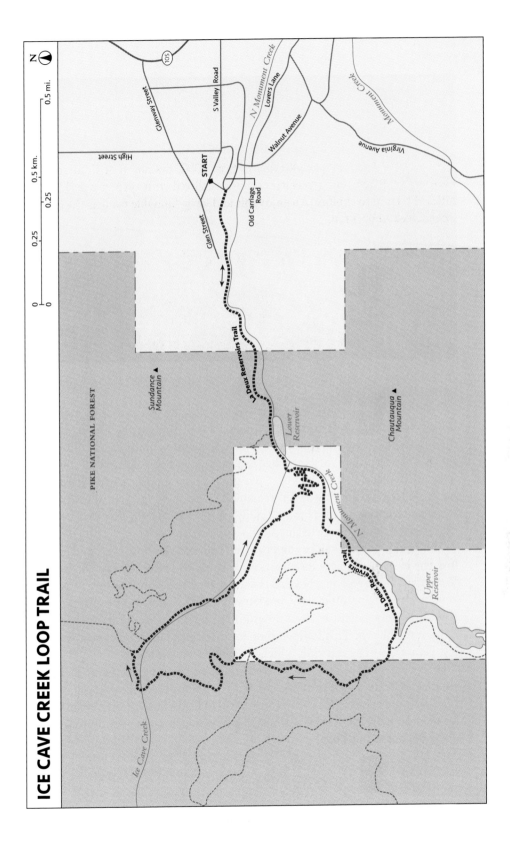

ICE CAVE CREEK LOOP TRAIL

N

0.5 mi.

0   0.25   0.5 km.

PIKE NATIONAL FOREST

Sundance Mountain ▲

Chautauqua Mountain ▲

La Deux Reservoirs Trail

La Deux Reservoirs Trail

Lower Reservoir

Upper Reservoir

N Monument Creek

N Monument Creek

Ice Cave Creek

Monument Creek

START

Glen Street

Old Carriage Road

S Valley Road

Glenway Street

High Street

Lovers Lane

Walnut Avenue

Virginia Avenue

105

Wide and sweeping vistas abound in Palmer Park.
PHOTO BY NANCY HOBBS

RUN DESCRIPTION

The route starts out on a wide, dirt road flanked on either side by trees. What may seem gentle to start becomes a steep climb at the outset, but then flattens out by the first reservoir. A few more climbs ensue, but in general, the terrain is very groomed and runnable, albeit slippery in some spots, with loose, ball-bearing-size pea gravel. The singletrack in the forest provides great footing and three quick creek crossings. Views include rocky outcroppings and, at the 3.0-mile point, a vista to the east that begs the runner to stop to take in the view.

This trail is not marked beyond the trailhead signage. Head west and follow the loop in a clockwise direction, keeping the reservoirs to the left. Turn right at the fork just beyond the second reservoir, and continue right at subsequent forks on mostly singletrack terrain. There is one questionable three-way juncture: Head downhill/straight at this point, about 1.8 miles into the run. This lollipop loop joins with the initial dirt roadway just before the first reservoir, which is visible from the trail.

Following your time spent on the trails, enjoy some snacks at Rock House Ice Cream, or coffee at Speed Trap. For a sumptuous meal, check out the Villa, and for excellent wings stop by O'Malley's Steak Pub. And don't miss the actually namesake—Palmer Lake—which boasts a great 18-basket disc golf course on its banks.

MOUNT HERMAN

AT JUST OVER 9,000 FEET, Mount Herman lies along the Rampart Range of the Front Range near the town of Monument, within the Pike National Forest. In addition to a trail (approximately 4 miles round-trip) to the summit from Mount Herman Road, there are trail opportunities at the base, providing connections to additional routes to the west, north, and south. There is also an 11-mile loop to the summit and back from the start point of the routes listed below. As well, the two routes below can also be joined by a singletrack trail connector for additional mileage.

MONUMENT ROCK LOOP

THE RUN DOWN

START: Trailhead at the Nursery Road parking lot; elevation 7,013 feet

OVERALL DISTANCE: 2.6-mile loop

APPROXIMATE RUNNING TIME: 27 minutes

DIFFICULTY: Green

ELEVATION GAIN: 205 feet

BEST SEASON TO RUN: Year-round

DOG FRIENDLY: Leashed dogs permitted

PARKING: Free

OTHER USERS: Equestrians; mountain bikers

CELL PHONE COVERAGE: Good

MORE INFORMATION: www.fs.usda.gov/recarea/ psicc/recreation/hiking/ recarea/?recid=27702& actid=50

FINDING THE TRAILHEAD

From I-25, take the Monument exit (#161/CO 105) and follow it west to 2nd Street. At the T, across from the railroad tracks, turn left on Mitchell Avenue, and then turn right on Mount Herman Road, located just before Dirty Woman Creek Park (named after a colorful—for her harsh demeanor and foul mouth—homesteader from the 1870s). Follow Mount Herman Road to Nursery Road, and the trailhead is by the parking lot on the west side of the road.

RUN DESCRIPTION

Take the northernmost track, which is a singletrack trail. Follow the gently rolling and smooth trail to a dirt road approximately 0.8 mile into the run. Turn left and pick up the singletrack on the other side of the road by a gate. After a short descent, there is a slight climb to the pond, named by locals "Stinky Pond" for obvious reasons. The pond sits adjacent to the aptly named Monument Rock, and another very small water feature known as "Guacamole Pond" due to its green tint. Views are outstanding of the foothills and Mount Herman to the west and the town of Monument to the east.

At Monument Rock, bear right to make this a complete and counter-clockwise loop, or circle Stinky Pond to make it a keyhole loop. The counterclockwise route on the singletrack reaches a dirt road (the same one crossed on the outbound journey, but farther south). Follow that north approximately 0.4 mile to a doubletrack connector on the right. Follow as this trail undulates back to the parking lot.

OVERLOOK TO MEMORIAL GROVE

THE RUN DOWN

START: Trailhead at the corner of Lindbergh Road and Schilling Avenue; elevation 7,041 feet

OVERALL DISTANCE: 2.2-mile loop

APPROXIMATE RUNNING TIME: 40 minutes

DIFFICULTY: Blue

ELEVATION GAIN: 354 feet

BEST SEASON TO RUN: Year-round

DOG FRIENDLY: Leashed dogs permitted

PARKING: Free

OTHER USERS: Equestrians; mountain bikers

CELL PHONE COVERAGE: Good

MORE INFORMATION: www.fs.usda.gov/recarea/ psicc/recreation/hiking/ recarea/?recid=27702& actid=50

FINDING THE TRAILHEAD

From I-25, take the Monument exit (#161/CO 105) and follow it west to 2nd Street. At the T, across from the railroad tracks, turn left on Mitchell Avenue, and then turn right on Mount Herman Road, located just before Dirty Woman Creek Park (named after a colorful—for her harsh demeanor and foul mouth—homesteader from the 1870s). Follow Mount Herman Road to Nursery Road. Continue south on Nursery Road to a dirt parking lot at the corner of Lindbergh Road and Schilling Avenue. The trailhead is just beyond the gate on the west side of the road.

RUN DESCRIPTION

Starting at the gate, head west on a wide dirt road. At the first junction, marked Forest Service Trail (FS) #715, turn left. This singletrack trail climbs to the high point of this route. Stay right at any junction on this route. Scrub oak flanks both sides of the trail, and exposed rocks require focus on the rolling terrain. After crossing the high point and enjoying the views, descend on the singletrack to a dirt road at Memorial Grove, an homage to firefighters. Follow the road back to the start point to finish this clockwise loop.

SPRUCE MOUNTAIN OPEN SPACE

LOCATED IN DOUGLAS COUNTY, this area boasts over 1,300 acres and 8.5 miles of well-marked trails. With forested sections, open meadows, and ridgetop vistas, this area is varied and diverse. Partners in the Spruce Mountain Open Space include Great Outdoors Colorado, The Conservation Fund, Douglas County, private conservation buyers, United States Department of Agriculture, and Colorado State Forest Service.

THE RUN DOWN

START: Trail starts at Spruce Mountain; elevation 7,130 feet

OVERALL DISTANCE: 5.25-mile loop

APPROXIMATE RUNNING TIME: 50 minutes

DIFFICULTY: Green

ELEVATION GAIN: 583 feet

BEST SEASON TO RUN: Year-round

DOG FRIENDLY: Leashed dogs permitted

PARKING: Free

OTHER USERS: Equestrians, mountain bikers

CELL PHONE COVERAGE: Good

MORE INFORMATION: www .douglas.co.us/dcoutdoors/ openspace-properties/spruce-mountain-open-space-and-trail/

FINDING THE TRAILHEAD

From I-25, take the Monument exit and follow CO 105 through the town of Palmer Lake to Spruce Mountain Road, which is located just north of the town's namesake: Palmer Lake. The parking lot is on the west side of Spruce Mountain Road. The trailhead is located on the west side of the parking lot just beyond the split rail fence.

RUN DESCRIPTION

Start on doubletrack trail for this 5.25-mile loop. Continue to the next trailhead, approximately 0.3 mile, and turn left on the Mountain Top Loop. Follow this singletrack, a smooth-surfaced trail complete with switchbacks and occasional roots and rocks, but nothing technical. Sections of the trail have loose sand to test ankle strength and stability. Enjoy spectacular views of the Greenland Open Space and the Palmer Divide to the north and east, and an occasional glimpse of Pikes Peak poking up in the distance to the southwest.

At the next junction, at approximately 1.6 miles, head in a clockwise direction to reach the far reaches of the trail to the south, at Windy Point. Here, enjoy nearly 360-degree views. Continue on the loop heading back to the junction and follow the trail back to the parking lot. On this route, the Oak shortcut at Pine Junction was chosen to reduce the loop by 0.2 mile.

GREENLAND OPEN SPACE

LOCATED IN DOUGLAS COUNTY, this 3,000-acre open space boasts 10 miles of trails mostly in open meadows, with views of Pikes Peak to the southwest and Spruce Mountain to the west. The Greenland Trail is part of the Front Range Trail, and connects south to the Santa Fe Trail and to the Spruce Mountain Trail to the west.

GREENLAND OPEN SPACE

THE RUN DOWN

START: Greenland trailhead; elevation 6,917 feet

OVERALL DISTANCE: 8.0-mile loop

APPROXIMATE RUNNING TIME: 70 minutes

DIFFICULTY: Green

ELEVATION GAIN: 486 feet

BEST SEASON TO RUN: Year-round

DOG FRIENDLY: Leashed dogs permitted

PARKING: Free

OTHER USERS: Equestrians, mountain bikers

CELL PHONE COVERAGE: Good

MORE INFORMATION: www .douglas.co.us/dcoutdoors/ trails/open-space-trails/6783-2/

FINDING THE TRAILHEAD

The open space is located just west of I-25, off the East Greenland Road exit (#167). Turn south on East Noe Road, and park in the gravel/dirt lot. There are restrooms near the trailhead at the pavilion.

RUN DESCRIPTION

Follow the trail south to the second junction, and turn right to head east (uphill). After several switchbacks, the trail turns north to run nearly parallel to the outbound trail. An equal amount of ascending and descending makes this an enjoyable loop. The route can be extended to the south to the town of Palmer Lake and points farther south.

PHILIP S. MILLER PARK

NEW TRAILS AND AMENITIES HAVE BEEN ADDED TO THIS 320-ACRE PARK since its opening in 2014. In addition to an extensive network of trails, there is a zip line, an adventure tower, playing fields, bungee jumping, and the 64,443-square-foot, two-story Miller Activity Complex, offering artificial turf fields for indoor soccer, lacrosse, and football, as well as an aquatics center. Trails are marked with colored arrows on signposts to indicate the loop corresponding with the trail map. Mostly singletrack, the trails are undulating and relatively smooth, with an equal amount of ascending and descending, sometimes including switchbacks as well as long, flat sections. Several races are annually staged on the trails, varying in length from 5K to 21K.

10K OF CONNECTING LOOPS

THE RUN DOWN

START: Paved path near the amphitheater; elevation 6,456 feet

OVERALL DISTANCE: 6.2 miles round-trip

APPROXIMATE RUNNING TIME: 60 minutes

DIFFICULTY: Blue

ELEVATION GAIN: 710 feet

BEST SEASON TO RUN: Year-round

DOG FRIENDLY: Leashed dogs permitted

PARKING: Free

OTHER USERS: Mountain bikers

CELL PHONE COVERAGE: Good

MORE INFORMATION: www .crgov.com/2051/Philip-S-Miller-Park

FINDING THE TRAILHEAD

From I-25, take exit #181/Plum Creek Parkway and head west. The park is on the south side of Plum Creek Parkway within 0.5 mile of the exit ramp. From the park entrance, keep right and continue to the last parking lot. This route starts near the amphitheater on the paved path. Head uphill on the pavement to join the Gold Loop Trail.

RUN DESCRIPTION

This route includes the Gold Loop and Purple Loop trails in Philip S. Miller Park, as well as trails in the 367-acre Ridgeline Open Space, accessed via a footbridge over West Wolfensberger Road. The Ridgeline Open Space trails are marked with small signs including the name of the trail. Trails are both singletrack and doubletrack, with the majority being the former. Carrying a map is advised to follow the chosen route. Both the Ridgeline Open Space and Philip S. Miller Park are with the jurisdiction of the city of Castle Rock. Views along the trail encompass the Front Range to the west and Castle Rock to the east.

COLORADO SPRINGS RUNS

10K ON LOWER LOOP TRAILS

THE RUN DOWN

START: On the pavement on the west side of the playing field; elevation 6,377 feet

OVERALL DISTANCE: 6.2-mile round-trip

APPROXIMATE RUNNING TIME: 55 minutes

DIFFICULTY: Blue

ELEVATION GAIN: 565 feet

BEST SEASON TO RUN: Year-round

DOG FRIENDLY: Leashed dogs permitted

PARKING: Free

OTHER USERS: Mountain bikers

CELL PHONE COVERAGE: Good

MORE INFORMATION: www .crgov.com/2051/Philip-S-Miller-Park

FINDING THE TRAILHEAD

From I-25, take exit #181/Plum Creek Parkway and head west. The park is on the south side of Plum Creek Parkway within 0.5 mile of the exit ramp. Start on the pavement on the west side of the playing field located south of the activity complex, and head south before turning west to join the Gold Loop Trail.

RUN DESCRIPTION

This run features many of the same trails as the 10K of Connecting Routes, with a short section on pavement and finishing at the sports field. This route includes most of the trail loops in the park, but does not utilize any of the trails in Ridgeline Open Space. The route is undulating, with gentle flat sections to provide a variety of terrain. Most of the route is in the open, providing excellent viewpoints throughout.

THE MINI-INCLINE

THE RUN DOWN

START: At the base of the steps on the east side of the park across from the infield; elevation 6,400 feet

OVERALL DISTANCE: 0.6 mile

APPROXIMATE RUNNING TIME: 8 minutes

DIFFICULTY: Blue

ELEVATION GAIN: 179 feet

BEST SEASON TO RUN: Year-round

DOG FRIENDLY: Leashed dogs permitted

PARKING: Free

OTHER USERS: Foot traffic only on the steps

CELL PHONE COVERAGE: Good

MORE INFORMATION: www
.crgov.com/2051/Philip-S-
Miller-Park

FINDING THE TRAILHEAD

From I-25, take exit #181/Plum Creek Parkway and head west. The park is on the south side of Plum Creek Parkway within 0.5 mile of the exit ramp. Start at the base of the steps located on the east side of the park across from the infield.

RUN DESCRIPTION

This lung-busting uphill climb features 200 wooden steps, equally spaced and numbered in 10-step increments. Reach the top and a short, flat, dirt and rocky section of trail past the Castle Rock Zip Line, and descend in several switchbacks down a singletrack trail. Test and repeat for a fitness challenge workout. When done with the mini-incline, take to the trails for a complete trail and stair-stepping adventure.

MANITOU SPRINGS

NESTLED NEAR THE EASTERN BASE OF PIKES PEAK—familiar to most and beloved by all as America's Mountain—sits the quiet and rustic city of Manitou Springs. The city is located just a few miles west of the border of the more sprawling and urban Colorado Springs. Because of its proximity to Pikes Peak, Manitou Springs offers an abundance of trails, including the ever-popular Barr Trail, which winds from Manitou to the 14,115-foot summit, and the outdoor Stairmaster workout afforded by the Incline, a nearly 1-mile climb up a route used until the 1990s as a funicular railway. In addition to these oxygen-depriving ascents, there are more mellow and rolling trails, as well as those with measurable elevation gain and awe-inspiring views.

IRON MOUNTAIN TRAIL

The Iron Mountain Trail is a 2.0-mile, out-and-back jaunt that boasts 971 feet of climbing and is perfect for an early morning or late afternoon pick-me-up workout. The run can also be part of a longer outing on the connecting Intemann Trail (memorializing Paul Intemann, a Manitou Springs city planner who died in a car crash in 1986), which runs about 5 miles from Red Rock Canyon Open Space, located on the outskirts of Colorado Springs, west to Manitou Springs.

THE RUN DOWN

START: The Iron Mountain/ Intemann trailhead; elevation 6,318 feet, approximately

OVERALL DISTANCE: 3.6 miles out and back

APPROXIMATE RUNNING TIME: 40 minutes

DIFFICULTY: Blue

ELEVATION GAIN: 971 feet

BEST SEASON TO RUN: Year-round

DOG FRIENDLY: Dogs must be on leash at all times

PARKING: None near the trailhead, as it is residential; park at the start in Manitou Springs

OTHER USERS: Hikers, bikers

CELL PHONE COVERAGE: Yes

MORE INFORMATION: http:// www.intemanntrail.com/ or http://www.fotp.com/8-trails/ fotp-trails/iron-mountain

FINDING THE TRAILHEAD

There is no parking at the trailhead, and very limited parking in the neighborhood near the trailhead, so it is best to park at Memorial Park in Manitou Springs, located at the corner of Manitou Avenue and El Paso, which is approximately 0.5 mile from the trailhead.

RUN DESCRIPTION

From the starting point at Memorial Park, head west on Manitou Avenue to Pawnee Street, and then head south, where the road becomes rather steep. Follow to the fork at Midland Avenue, and continue on up Pawnee,

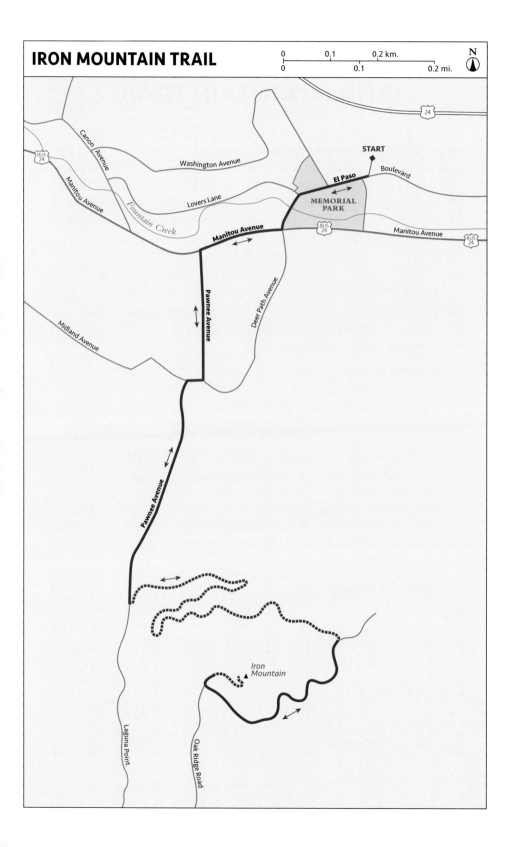

IRON MOUNTAIN TRAIL

0   0.1   0.2 km.

0   0.1   0.2 mi.

N

Canon Avenue

Washington Avenue

BUS 24

Manitou Avenue

Lovers Lane

Fountain Creek

START

El Paso   Boulevard

MEMORIAL PARK

Manitou Avenue

BUS 24

Manitou Avenue

BUS 24

24

Manitou Avenue

Pawnee Avenue

Deer Path Avenue

Midland Avenue

Pawnee Avenue

Iron Mountain

Laguna Point

Oak Ridge Road

On the Iron Mountain Trail with US 24 in the distance. PHOTO BY TIM BERGSTEN

where a sign indicates a dead end. Climb less than 0.25 mile and the trailhead is on the east side of the street.

The trail is wide enough in spots to run two abreast, but is primarily singletrack in design. Once on the trail, there is only one fork, with the north track heading to the summit of Iron Mountain, and the south track heading to the Intemann Trail and Red Rock Canyon Open Space. Stay on the north track to Iron Mountain.

The trail surface is generally smooth and mostly dirt, with patches of grass in spots and a few rocky spots requiring eyes on the trail to navigate. A few gentle switchbacks and a decent amount of climbing—roughly 900 feet—make this a short but challenging run. The views are outstanding, and overlook Manitou Springs to the north and west, and Colorado Springs to the east. Glimpses of the Incline and Pikes Peak are afforded from the top of Iron Mountain.

This trail can be run year-round in trail shoes without the need for traction devices unless there is heavy snowfall. Most of the trail is out in the open, with few shady sections. Avoid the trail in heavy thunderstorms or when lightning is imminent.

Following your run, visit the Colorado Custard Company in downtown Manitou Springs for a sundae or a sandwich, where you may be greeted by shop owner, Matt Carpenter, a local running legend and Pikes Peak Marathon course record holder. For a more relaxing post-run treat, visit the SunWater Spa, or rejuvenate your muscles with a soak in the Fountain Creek, which runs east/west through town.

And if you haven't gotten enough time on your feet, enjoy a walking tour of the eight natural mineral springs in town, and sample the free and fresh flowing water. Stop by the visitor center on the east edge of town to pick up a map or join a group for a more in-depth educational experience. Stop in at one of the many shops to purchase locally made pottery, artwork, or a custom-designed T-shirt, all within walking distance in downtown.

If it's a post-run brew you're after, Manitou Brewing Company and Kinfolks are great watering holes. If your palette prefers margaritas and Mexican food, try the Loop. For more good eats, head a bit east to Adam's Mountain Cafe, which relocated in 2014 from downtown Manitou Springs to 26 Manitou Avenue when repeated flooding after the Waldo Canyon Fire forced the owners to seek a venue away from the creek. The fire burned more than 18,000 acres and destroyed 346 homes in 2013, and several popular trails, including the Waldo Canyon Loop on scenic US 24, remain closed to this day.

BARR TRAIL/ MANITOU INCLINE

ONCE A SCENIC UPHILL RAILWAY, the Manitou Incline is now a popular outdoor fitness destination for its steep ascent, gaining nearly 2,000 feet in less than 1 mile, and for the fantastic views from the top of its railroad-tie steps. Opened to the public in 2013, the Incline/Barr Trail route attracts as many as 1,500 visitors per day. The Barr Trail ascends some 7,800 feet from its base to the summit of Pikes Peak at 14,115 feet, on mostly singletrack trail.

INCLINE LOOP

THE RUN DOWN

START: At the base of the Incline steps; elevation 6,600 feet

OVERALL DISTANCE: 3.5-mile loop

APPROXIMATE RUNNING TIME: 90 minutes

DIFFICULTY: Black

ELEVATION GAIN: 2,000 feet

BEST SEASON TO RUN: Year-round, though the trail can get slick in winter

DOG FRIENDLY: No dogs allowed

PARKING: Parking is available for a fee on Ruxton Ave and at the Barr Trailhead, but with limited parking slots, the lot fills quickly

OTHER USERS: None

CELL PHONE COVERAGE: Fair

MORE INFORMATION: www.inclinefriends.org/

FINDING THE TRAILHEAD

From US 24, take the Manitou Springs exit and follow Manitou Avenue west to Ruxton Avenue, which is located at the roundabout.

Follow Ruxton to Hydro Street, and park at the Barr Trailhead lot if there is space. Parking is at a premium in Manitou Springs, and you will pay for the privilege of a spot near the Incline. Seasonally, park at the Tajine Alami Restaurant lot and take the free shuttle to the Incline. The start of the route is at the base of the Incline steps.

RUN DESCRIPTION

Make no mistake, this is not an easy route. The steep climb from the base of the Incline to the top is more hiking than running. Along the ascent, there is a false summit to play with your depth perception as well as your mental strength. Fear not: Continue up the steps until you crest the true summit and enjoy the accomplishment as well as the outstanding view from whence you came.

From the summit of the Incline steps, follow the marked trail south to Barr Trail. If you want extra mileage, continue to Barr Camp another 3 miles up—or go higher, to the summit of Pikes Peak 6 miles farther. If you have had enough ascending, turn left to return down the winding and often technical trail to the trailhead parking lot.

For another challenging run, consider the Ute Indian Trail, which is located to the north of the base of the Incline. Run an out-and-back route, or loop to Long's Ranch Road to join the Barr Trail for a nearly 11-mile loop (more information at www.inclineclub.com/maps/upt_lrr_bt.htm).

ATRA RULES ON THE RUN

"Rules on the Run" are principles of trail running etiquette that foster environmentally sound and socially responsible trail running. These principles emulate the well-established principles of Leave No Trace (https://lnt.org), and Rules of the Trail (www.imba.com/about/trail_rules.html) by the International Mountain Biking Association (IMBA). The American Trail Running Association (ATRA; www.trailrunner.com), believes that by educating trail runners to observe Rules on the Run, they will be able to enjoy continued access to their favorite trails and trail running competitions.

1. **Stay on the Trail:** Well-marked trails already exist; they are not made on the day you head out for a run, (i.e., making your own off-trail path). There is nothing cool about running off trail, bushwhacking over and under trees, or cutting switchbacks up the side of a hill or mountain. Such running creates new trails, encourages others to follow in your footsteps (creating unmarked "social trails"), and increases the runner's footprint on the environment. When multiple trails exist, run on the one that is the most worn. Stay off closed trails and obey all posted regulations.

2. **Run over obstacles:** Run single file in the middle of a trail, even when muddy or laden with a fresh blanket of snow. Go through puddles and not around them. Running around mud, rocks, or downed tree limbs widens trails, impacts vegetation, and causes further and unnecessary erosion. Use caution when going over obstacles, but challenge yourself by staying in the middle of the trail. If the terrain is exceedingly muddy, refrain from running on the trails so that you don't create damaging "potholes" in the surface. Moisture is the chief factor that determines how traffic (from any user group) affects a trail. For some soil types, a 100-pound runner can wreak havoc on a trail surface in extremely wet conditions. In dry conditions the same trail might easily withstand a 1,200-pound horse/rider combination. There are many situational factors to consider when making your trail running decision. Trails that have been constructed with rock work, or those with soils that drain quickly, may hold up to wet conditions—even a downpour. But, in general, if the trail is wet enough to become muddy and hold puddles all user groups should avoid it until the moisture has drained.

3. **Run Only on Officially Designated Open Trails:** Respect trail and road closures and avoid trespassing on private land. Get permission first to enter and run on private land. Obtain permits or authorizations that may be required for some wilderness areas and managed trail systems. Leave gates as you've found them. If you open a gate, be sure to close it behind you. Make sure the trails you run on are officially designated routes, not user-created routes. When in doubt, ask the land managing agency or individuals responsible for the area you are using.

4. **Respect Animals:** Do not disturb or harass wildlife or livestock. Animals scared by your sudden approach may be dangerous. Give them plenty of room to adjust to you. Avoid trails that cross known wildlife havens during sensitive times such as nesting or mating seasons. When passing horses use special care and follow directions from the horseback riders. Running cattle is a serious offense. Consider turning around and going another direction when faced with disturbing large herds of animals, especially in winter when animals are highly stressed already.

5. **Keep Your Dog on a Leash:** Unless otherwise posted, keep your dog on a leash and under control at all times. Dogs running off-leash may result in adverse impacts on terrain and wildlife and degrade the outdoor experience of other trail users. If an area is posted "No Dogs," obey signage. This may mean that you leave your dog at home. It is also imperative that you exercise Leave No Trace practices with respect to removing any dog waste, packing out what your dog may leave on the trail. Be prepared with a plastic bag and carry the waste until you come across a proper disposal receptacle.

6. **Don't Startle Other Trail Users:** A quick-moving trail runner, especially one who seemingly emerges from out of nowhere on an unsuspecting trail user, can be quite alarming. Give a courteous and audible announcement well in advance of your presence and intention to pass hikers on the trail, stating something like, "On your left," or "Trail" as you approach the trail users. Keep in mind your announcement doesn't work well for those who are wearing headphones and blasting music. Show respect when passing, by slowing down or stopping if necessary to prevent accidental contact. Be ready to yield to all other trail users (bikers, hikers, horses) even if you have the posted right of way. Uphill runners yield to downhill runners in most situations.

7. **Be Friendly:** The next step after not startling fellow users is letting them know they have a friend on the trail. Friendly communication is the key when trail users are yielding to one another. A "Thank you" is fitting when others on the trail yield to you. A courteous, "Hello, how are you?" shows kindness, which is particularly welcome.

8. **Don't Litter:** Pack out at least as much as you pack in. Gel wrappers with their little torn-off tops and old water bottles don't have a place on the trail. Consider wearing apparel with pockets that zip or a hydration pack that has a place to secure litter you find on the trail. Learn and use minimum impact techniques to dispose of human waste.

9. **Run in Small Groups:** Split larger groups into smaller groups. Larger groups can be very intimidating to hikers and have a greater environmental impact on trails. Most trail systems, parks, and wilderness areas have limits on group size. Familiarize yourself with the controlling policy and honor it.

10. **Safety:** Know the area you plan to run in and let at least one other person know where you are planning to run and when you expect to return. Run with a buddy if possible. Take a map with you in unfamiliar areas. Be prepared for the weather and conditions prevailing when you start your run and plan for the worst, given the likely duration of your run. Carry plenty of water, electrolyte replacement drink, or snacks for longer runs. Rescue efforts can be treacherous in remote areas. ATRA does not advise the use of headphones or iPods. The wearer typically hears nothing around them, including approaching wildlife, and other humans. The most important safety aspect is to know and respect your limits. Report unusually dangerous, unsafe, or damaging conditions and activities to the proper authorities.

11. **Leave What You Find:** Leave natural or historic objects as you find them. This includes wildflowers and native grasses. Removing or collecting trail markers is serious vandalism that puts others at risk.

12. **Giving Back:** Volunteer, support, and encourage others to participate in trail maintenance days.

TRAIL RACE ETIQUETTE FOR THE RACE DIRECTOR AND COMPETITOR

A few runners simply running on a trail normally have limited negative impacts. All the associated happenings of a trail race "event" add up and contribute to the total impact.

PREPARING FOR THE RACE AND SELECTING A COURSE

1. Involve the community. Make sure you secure all permits, permissions, and insurance. Cooperation from government officials (which may include parks departments, USDA Forest Service, etc.) is a must. Be mindful of potential trail conflicts with other users, which may include hikers, bikers, equestrians, or hunters. Let other public trail and area users know of your event in advance by using the media, postings at trailheads, etc., so that they have a chance to avoid the area during your race and are not surprised by the presence of runners on race day.

2. Select a race course that uses officially designated open public trails. Trail runners may want to test the course before and after the event. Using existing trails has another benefit: the trail bed should be well-established, durable, and firm. If you are using private trails or going through areas that are normally off limits, let runners know this in advance and strongly discourage them from using the route except on race day. Encourage your race participants to familiarize themselves with the race route only as much as is minimally necessary. Many popular race trails get "loved to death" during training by runners.

3. If existing trails don't offer the mileage or distance you would like to have as part of your course, or the type of elevation gains or losses you need, adjust your race distance to accommodate what already exists. ATRA suggests you always use existing trails rather than creating social trails, or detours.

4. Think about spectator, crew, and media movement around the course. This can often cause more damage than actual racing. Post signs to direct spectators to other course sections via established paths.

5. Limit the total number of participants allowed in your event in advance. Do not be greedy and blindly accept the number of entrants you might get. Work with land managing agencies to set a number that you, your staff, and the surrounding environment, trails, and facilities can safely accommodate with limited impact. Strive for quality of runner experience first, and quantity of runners later only if increased numbers can be accepted comfortably.

6. Consider encouraging carpooling to your race by allocating preferential parking areas to vehicles with three or more runners, giving cash "gas money" incentives to those runners that carpool, etc.

7. Realize that most people visiting the natural area where your trail race will be held are visiting that area primarily to experience natural

sights, sounds, and smells. Most trail race participants value these experiences also. Carefully consider how any "additions" to your event will impact and modify the natural experience for your race participants and others. Do you really need amplified music at the start, finish, and aid stations? Will everyone appreciate cheering spectators? Are banners and mileage markers necessary? Can one course official silently standing at an intersection pointing the way take the place of numerous flagging and ground markings?

8. Consider the timing of your event so as not to conflict with other trail and area users during already heavily used time periods. Scheduling your event in the off-season may avoid potential conflicts.

9. Plan and position your aid stations to minimize conflicts with other users and to avoid environmental impacts. Locate them in areas where access is easy, durable, or previously disturbed surfaces already exist, and away from areas favored by other users (campgrounds, fishing spots, picnic areas, etc.).

10. Plan your start/finish area with care. Is there adequate parking? Will heavy concentrated use damage the vegetation or land? Do restrooms already exist or can they be brought in and removed easily? Is there a wide enough trail (or better yet a road) for the first part of the race to allow the field to spread out and runners to pass before they separate enough to allow safe use of a singletrack trail?

11. If trail or start/finish/aid area conditions cannot accommodate your race without environmental damage (due to mud, high water, downed trees, etc.), consider canceling, rescheduling, or having an alternative route in place for your event.

12. Encourage electronic registration. Post your event entry forms online instead of printing and distributing thousands, or at least print entry forms on recycled paper.

DURING THE RACE

1. Mark the course with eco-friendly markings. These markings may include flour or cake mix (devil's food is great for courses run on snow), colored construction marking tape, paper plates hung on trees with directional arrows, flagging. Remove all markings immediately following the race, but be sure your markers are still in place at race time so runners do not go off course.

2. Provide a large course map at the start/registration area so runners can familiarize themselves with the trail.

3. Don't allow participants to run with their dogs on the course. This is a safety issue for other participants and for the dogs. Dogs also have been known to tow runners to an unfair advantage in a race.

4. Use the race as an opportunity to educate runners and spectators about responsible trail running. Include information about responsible training and volunteerism in each racer's entry packet. If you have a race announcer, provide him or her with a variety of short public messages that talk about responsible use of trails, joining a trail running club, and volunteering to maintain trails.

5. Encourage local trail advocacy organizations to share their information with the public at your event. If the race includes a product expo, allow local advocacy groups to exhibit without charge.

6. Green the event. Provide adequate portable toilets, drinking water, and trash receptacles. Let runners know where these will be located in advance. Recycle all cans, bottles, paper, and glass. Consider recyclable materials for awards and organic T-shirts for participants. Event organizers and all participants will benefit if they are seen as being at the forefront of energy and materials conservation. As a participant, carry a water bottle and refill at the aid station so you are not using extra cups. As a race director, consider requiring participants to start the race with their own fluid and food in a container (water bottle or pack) so as to eliminate the need for cups along the trail. Pack out your gel wrappers and trash. You as the participant should be responsible for your trash.

7. Limit spectator and crew access to points along the course that can safely accommodate them and their vehicles without damage. Consider prohibiting all spectator and crew access to the trail to preserve the trail experience for the participants and to limit impacts.

8. Promote local recreational trail running by making sure that maps, guidebooks, and brochures are available at the race. Involve local schoolchildren in the event in a kids' run if you have the resources.

9. Stop to help others in need, even while racing, and sacrifice your own event to aid other trail users who might be in trouble.

10. ATRA suggests participants refrain from using iPods/headphones in races. This is foremost a safety issue. Many running insurance providers do not permit use of these devices.

11. When you have two-way traffic, slower runners yield to faster runners, and on ascent/descents, the uphill runner should yield to the downhill runner.

12. Try to be patient when you are part of a conga line on crowded racing trails. Instead of creating social trails by passing a runner above or below the marked trail, yell out, "Trail," and "to your left" or "to your right." If you are the slower runner, stop and step aside to make it easier for the faster runner to overtake you.
13. ATRA does not condone bandit runners (unregistered runners). Not only are bandits a serious safety and liability concern for the race director, often there are limits in races set forth by a permit. Bandits can jeopardize the issuance of future permits.
14. Require runners to follow all race rules, including staying on the designated marked route, packing out everything they started the race with, not having crew/pacers/spectators on the route, etc. Send a strong statement by disqualifying those runners that do not follow the rules.

AFTER THE RACE

1. Do a thorough job of cleaning the start-finish area, parking lots, and repairing and restoring the trails used for the event. Leave the trails in better shape than they were in prior to the race. Document your restoration work with photos.
2. If your event has been financially successful, make a contribution to your local trail running advocacy group and, if possible, to ATRA, too. When you do this, send press releases announcing your donations. This will enhance your image in the local community.
3. Get a capable runner to run sweep of your entire race route as soon as possible after the event. This runner can pick up trash, course markings, note any trail damage that needs to be mitigated, gauge reaction from other trail users they encounter, as well as act as a safety net. This runner should carry a pack, cell phone, first aid kit, etc.

ROAD RUNNERS CLUB OF AMERICA (RRCA) GENERAL RUNNING SAFETY TIPS

- **Don't wear headphones.** Use your ears to be aware of your surroundings. Your ears may help you avoid dangers your eyes may miss during evening or early morning runs.
- **Run against traffic so you can observe approaching automobiles.** By facing oncoming traffic, you may be able to react quicker than if it is behind you.
- **Look both ways before crossing.** Be sure the driver of a car acknowledges your right-of-way before crossing in front of a vehicle. Obey traffic signals.
- **Carry identification or write your name, phone number, and blood type on the inside sole of your running shoe.** Include any important medical information.
- **Always stay alert and aware of what's going on around you.** The more aware you are, the less vulnerable you are.
- **Carry a cell phone or change for a phone call.** Know the locations of public phones along your regular route.
- **Trust your intuition about a person or an area.** React on your intuition and avoid a person or situation if you're unsure. If something tells you a situation is not "right," it isn't.
- **Alter or vary your running route pattern; run in familiar areas if possible.** In unfamiliar areas, such as while traveling, contact a local RRCA club or running store. Know where open businesses or stores are located in case of emergency.
- **Run with a partner.** Run with a dog.
- **Write down or leave word of the direction of your run.** Tell friends and family of your favorite running routes.
- **Avoid unpopulated areas, deserted streets, and overgrown trails.** Avoid unlit areas, especially at night. Run clear of parked cars or bushes.
- **Ignore verbal harassment and do not verbally harass others.** Use discretion in acknowledging strangers. Look directly at others and be observant, but keep your distance and keep moving.
- **Wear reflective material if you must run before dawn or after dark.** Avoid running on the street when it is dark.
- **Practice memorizing license tags or identifying characteristics of strangers.**

- **Carry a noisemaker.** Get training in self-defense.
- **When using multiuse trails, follow the rules of the road.** If you alter your direction, look over your shoulder before crossing the trail to avoid a potential collision with an oncoming cyclist or passing runner.
- **Call police immediately if something happens to you or someone else, or you notice anyone out of the ordinary.** It is important to report incidents immediately.

USEFUL WEBSITES

- www.trailrunner.com
- www.trailrunproject.com
- www.strava.com
- www.trailsandopenspaces.org
- www.rrca.org
- www.bouldercolorado.gov
- www.boulderrunning.com
- www.bouldertrails.org
- http://jeffco.us/open-space/parks/
- www.ci.westminster.co.us/ParksRec/TrailSystem/
- http://highlandsranch.org/services/parks-open-space/trails/
- www.gardenofthegods.com
- www.cospringstrails.com/
- www.cheyennecanon.org
- www.townofpalmerlake.com/
- www.manitoucats.com/
- http://cpw.state.co.us/placestogo/Parks/cheyennemountain